RESTORATION RECIPES

Julia de Bierre & James Bain Smith

Location photography by Bill Batten
Studio photography by Patrick McLeavey

Quadrille

To Shirley, Max, Corisande and Tim, who helped us in so many ways

p. 1: *Corner detail of a French 19th-century mirror, showing both oil and water gilding*

pp. 2–3: *Rosewood veneered drawers on a late 17th-century collector's cabinet, complete with secret compartments*

p. 4: *Restored edge of a painted and patinated washstand*

p. 5: *Late 18th-century Louis Seize armchair, in carved and painted beech*

The publisher takes no responsibility for any injury or loss arising from the procedures or materials described in this book. Materials, tools, skills, and work areas vary greatly and are the responsibility of the reader. Follow the manufacturers' instructions and take the appropriate safety precautions.

Art Director Mary Evans
Publishing Director Jane O'Shea
Art Editor Sue Storey
Project Editor Mary Davies
Editor Nicki Marshall

Picture Researcher Sara-Jane Glyn
Assistant Designer Lisbet Tonner
Photographic Assistant Andi Barker
Production Julie Hadingham and Vincent Smith

This paperback edition first published in 2005 by Quadrille Publishing Limited Alhambra House, 27–31 Charing Cross Road, London WC2H OLS

British Library Cataloguing-in-Publication Data
A catalogue record for this book is available from the British Library.

ISBN-13: 978 184400 278 8
ISBN-10: 1 84400 278 0

Printed and bound in Spain

CONTENTS

6   Introduction
8   Where to purchase
10   What to look out for

12   **PART ONE – GETTING STARTED**
14   Understanding wood
22   Before you begin
24   Tools and materials
36   Infestation and rot
38   Cleaning and stripping
43   Consolidation
67   Metal fittings
72   Upholstery

80   **PART TWO – SURFACES**
82   Surface repairs
88   Veneer repairs
94   French polishing
100   Working with gesso and gilding
108   Painted, stained and waxed finishes

124   **PART THREE – PROJECTS**

172   List of suppliers
173   Index
176   Acknowledgments

INTRODUCTION

This is a book for furniture enthusiasts, for all those who share our love for the well-worn antique or second-hand piece and who wish to progress to the rewarding practicalities of restoration work. The motivation may be financial – furniture found in a less than perfect state is much more affordable than its undamaged counterpart – or it may be some need for the simple satisfaction to be won from working by hand, using time-honoured methods and materials.

The knowledge we share with you in *Restoration Recipes* is inspired in part by experience gained while running hands-on furniture restoration and decorative arts courses in the extraordinary setting of the Château de Lucens every year. We would like to think that the carefully researched and tested information gathered here is an accessible, coherent response to many of the problems encountered by the amateur restorer – whether beginner or more experienced.

Our design and restoration work for private clients and collectors has meant that we too have caught that seductive collecting 'bug'. Over the years we have accumulated an interesting assortment of furniture: some are *bona fide* antiques, some are 'in the style of', while others fall into the category of what a smart antique-dealer friend unkindly calls 'decorative debris'. What all these pieces have in common, aesthetics apart, is that each was in need of restoration and hence was just right for a tiny budget. Coaxing furniture back to life using traditional methods requires time, thought and patience, but when we survey the results, knowing that they will last, it is clear that the process was not just hugely enjoyable but well worth the effort.

The glow of wax-polished wood sets off the plain lines of Shaker furniture. Although original pieces are hard to come by, the Shaker concepts of utility and simplicity have contributed to our appreciation of natural wood finishes.

An increasing appreciation of old furniture, and an awareness of how it can improve with age, means that the whole concept of restoration has changed radically over the last two decades. We now know that old patina and original paintwork should be retained where possible, that the odd dent or blemish does not detract from the beauty of a piece, that repairs should be reversible and replacement parts kept to a minimum. Gone are the bad old days when restoration meant renovation or, even worse, transformation. We want antiques to look what they are – old – and not bland and gleaming.

This 17th-century chest, with locking grille doors, was originally designed for an apothecary. Fantasy marbling enhanced with gold leaf brings richness and colour to a pine carcase. Centuries of candle grease and smoke have darkened the paint but cleaning would reveal a strident green – an instance where we would 'leave well alone'. The chair, of the same period, was re-upholstered in antique velvet.

Museum conservation departments have been partially responsible for this new age of enlightenment. Their highly qualified specialists are now far more communicative, and the conservators' twin precepts of stabilizing past deterioration and protecting from future damage rather than undertaking major overhauls have filtered down to the general public. Restoration is as much about an attitude, or even a philosophy, as it is about manual activity.

By following the simple principles outlined here, you will master the basic skills needed before you can graduate to more complex pieces. Very valuable furniture in need of attention should, of course, be left to a professional restorer – if in doubt as to the nature of your piece, always consult an expert. We hope that this book will convey the rich diversity of restoration, which encompasses so many crafts and centuries of tradition. We hope too that it will reflect our passion for furniture in all its guises and that the thrill and exhilaration we have in resuscitating pieces seemingly past redemption will prove inspirational.

WHERE TO PURCHASE

A solid mahogany 19th-century chair (c. 1820) in need of major restoration work: its riotous springs were a later addition and are inappropriate for the style of the piece. They should be removed and the original, stuff-over seat reinstated (see page 72).

When buying antique and second-hand furniture, it is essential to start with an informed approach: read as much as you can about the styles that appeal to you and train your eye by visiting museums and collections. If possible, try to see furniture *in situ* – museums such as the Metropolitan Museum in New York display whole room sets which really make the pieces come alive. Even if you will never own such furniture, you will find by looking – really looking – at the ultimate in design and craftsmanship you will learn to recognize the sub-standard period piece or the thin, mean copy. Invest in good reference books (try second-hand bookshops for reasonable prices) and collect back numbers of auction catalogues, however minor (you can find them second-hand too): a lot can be learnt from the clear photographs, detailed descriptions and estimated prices. The huge diversity of styles featured in auction catalogues is also a great way for you to begin forming your own preferences.

Our passion for tracking down interesting old pieces at accessible prices means that finds usually need restoration. In antique shops furniture tends to be already restored, and this is inevitably reflected in the price. Regular visits to junk shops and tail ends of flea markets pay dividends *if* you can do the repairs yourself. These places are generally the end of the road for damaged but potentially appealing pieces.

It takes motivation and imagination to sift through depressingly dusty piles of broken chair legs and warped, useless-looking boards but persevere. If you remember, for example, that wood looks terrible when uncared for but will respond beautifully to careful cleaning and polish, you will soon be as hooked as we are. Many of the projects we discuss were found in this way.

Minor auction-house sales are also a good source because lower estimates are given for furniture that needs repair and 'job lots' can include some real finds that have mysteriously slipped through the net. Fix your ceiling price before the sale – auction-room fever is notoriously catching and it is all too easy to get carried away once bidding starts.

Much of the furniture you find to restore will probably date from the mid-19th century, possibly in one of the 'Revival' styles. Although purists might recoil in horror, changing aesthetic tastes and a refreshing indifference to the 'stylistically correct' means that these pieces, if solid and well made, are now thought to be worthy of attention: Gothic Revival, for example, is highly collectable.

Affordable pieces can also be found in the style known as Country or Provincial, both generic terms loosely used in the trade to indicate pieces made by a country or provincial-town carpenter or joiner as opposed to the city-based cabinet maker or *ébéniste*. These are often simplified interpretations of the more sophisticated designs of the day, made out of local woods and incorporating local decorative features. Dating such furniture is difficult since changes in style and construction were often slower than in the cities: in France, for example, country carpenters or *menuisiers* continued making Rococo right up until 1800.

As we enter the 21st century, the definition of 'antique' has become increasingly elastic. Pieces designed in the 1960s, '70s and even '80s now feature in auctions, often fetching high prices for prototypes or one-offs. Furniture is once again being seen as a potential work of art and not purely as functional equipment.

With experience you will acquire a 'nose' for bargains and for where to find them. Dark, dusty corners can yield treasures but try to look at potential pieces under good lighting before paying the quoted price.

WHAT TO LOOK OUT FOR

When it comes to recognizing a potential bargain at the flea market or auction house, nothing beats having had to dismantle a chair or table for restoration purposes, analyze its parts, date them (sometimes they can span several centuries), and then restore the piece with the materials and tools of the type used when the piece was first made. Knowing how to use a chisel or a handsaw, and the sort of marks these tools make, is invaluable when appraising that decorative 19th-century machine-made desk that the antique dealer insists is 18th century – and has priced accordingly!

To date a piece and distinguish antiques from reproductions or fakes, you need not just an in-depth knowledge of historical styles and construction techniques but powers of deduction worthy of a detective. There are a number of questions you should ask yourself when assessing any piece of 'period' furniture. What style is it? What is its country of origin? Do the decorative motifs correspond to the given style? Was this furniture in use at that time? (There's no such thing as an 18th-century low coffee table!) What woods are used? Were they used during that period? How thick is the veneer? (Rule of thumb: the thicker the veneer, the older the piece.) Are there differences in patina? Watch out for grey patinas and for furniture that has been varnished or painted in places hidden from view, i.e. at the back of drawers. Are there logical signs of wear on the piece? (Fakers often hit furniture randomly with chains and stones.) And remember: worm holes are impossible to duplicate artificially – take a magnifying glass and look for signs of tools around the edge of the hole.

SPOTTING THE COPY

Examination of two 18th-century style chairs.

Chair A The inner seat rail clearly shows the slight unevenness characteristic of handsaw marks. Note also how the angle of the cut changes pitch at the curves as the craftsman 'turns the corner' with his saw. Also, since sandpaper did not exist in the 18th century, difficult corners are rough to the touch.

Chair B There is no attempt to hide machine marks. The identical, parallel lines are typical of a bandsaw's cutting edge; the cushion rebate has been shaped with a rotating cutter (note the scribed curves at front of the cut). The smooth underside was achieved with a sander. **Verdict:** Chair A dates from the 18th century; chair B is a late 19th-century copy.

Two French chests, both of high quality and in Régence (early 18th-century) style.

Chest A This chest has a burl walnut veneer, seldom used during the Régence period. The bronze fittings are all identically regular, without the usual casting flaws found in the early 18th century. The marble top, also an unusual feature, has the same thickness all the way round, and the back is smooth, indicating a machine-made piece.

Chest B The thick (3mm) rosewood veneer on a pine carcase and the veneered panel covering the entire top demonstrate details typical of the Régence period. The bronze fittings, although finely chased, show irregularities indicative of hand tooling.

Drawer construction On B (*bottom*) the back panel creates or 'meets' the corner – note how it overlaps the side panel at its upper edge. This is called 'sailing through' and is typical of construction prior to 1840. The dovetails are uneven, indicating hand cutting. On A (*top*) it is the side panel that 'meets' the corner – in other words, the overlap has been reversed – indicating a piece made post-1840.

Verdict: B is a genuine Régence *commode*; A is a good 19th-century copy.

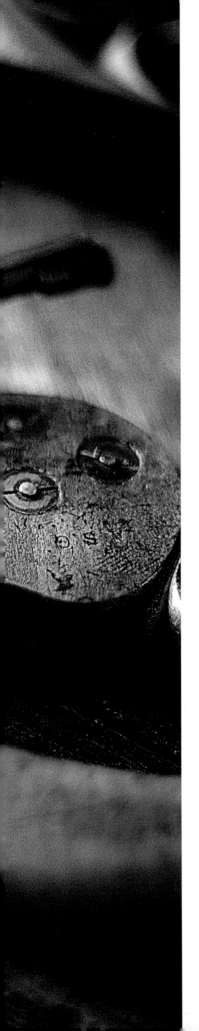

PART ONE

GETTING STARTED

A guide to the essential preliminaries of restoration: the different woods you may encounter, the tools and materials you will be working with, combating infestation and rot, and the best ways to clean surfaces before restoration work can begin, plus step-by-step accounts of how to deal with common structural problems found on antique chairs, tables and chests of drawers, how to repair or replace damaged or missing metal fittings, and how to effect simple upholstery repairs

Many of the tools we use in restoration are themselves antiques and superb objects in their own right. We love the solid beauty of our ebony and brass-inlay mortise gauge, made 100 years ago, and this 80-year old steel tenon saw, which never seems to need sharpening. It is still surprisingly easy to find second-hand tools (see page 24) and a great way to build up an inexpensive, top-quality tool chest.

UNDERSTANDING WOOD

In this brief section we hope to give you some understanding of how the various types of wood used in cabinet making are formed, where and how to buy wood, how it behaves, and how to identify the woods you are likely to come across in restoration. The tree is one of the most important parts of our eco-system, providing oxygen and verdant beauty for an increasingly polluted planet. It is vital to treat wood with all the respect that is its due – it is a finite supply and your restoration work, which hopefully will involve the use of salvaged or re-cycled timbers, should not contribute to the depletion of the forests.

IDENTIFYING WOOD

This is one of the essential tasks facing the restorer, a task complicated by the fact that no two trees are identical, even if of the same species. The effects of time or manufactured stains can change the surface appearance quite radically, and different cutting methods can produce varying grain patterns and colours. Even the most experienced craftsman can make mistakes. If the wood is solid, it is helpful to look underneath the piece of furniture to see it in its natural state.

Of the more than 70,000 different species of tree known to man you will, perhaps thankfully, only encounter a very limited selection. The charts on pages 18–21 should give you guidance in identifying some of the woods you are most likely to meet in restoration.

The timber trade divides wood under two main headings: softwood and hardwood. This is a somewhat perverse nomenclature since certain softwoods are a great deal harder than hardwood and vice versa: who would think that balsa-wood is a hardwood? The distinction refers to the structure of the wood; broadly speaking, softwoods are represented by conifers with needle-shaped leaves and naked seeds, and hardwoods by trees with broad leaves and cased seeds. In our charts, numbers 1–11 are classified as hardwoods, 12–13 softwoods, and 14–16 'exotics'.

BUYING WOOD FOR RESTORATION

Ideally a tree should be felled at the time of year when the sap flows the least, and it should be fully mature. An oak, for example, may be considered mature at the venerable age of between 60 and 100 years old. Nowadays, trees tend to be cut as soon as they are of moderate size and the important seasoning process which should slowly dry out remaining sap is often artificially speeded up by kiln drying, as opposed to the traditional method of air drying, which could take many years. The resulting timber does not always have the stability of vintage woods and is prone to warp and buckle. Taking into account ecological considerations, this is another good reason for re-cycling wood.

Architectural salvage yards provide a good source of old floor boards and broken-up panelling which can be used for solid-wood repairs, while junk shops will occasionally turn up seriously damaged pieces of furniture known in the trade as 'breakers' because they defy even the most accomplished restorer but can be broken up for spare parts or veneer replacements. For highly visible repairs it is worth the search since old wood has a colour and patination difficult to reproduce.

If you do have to buy new wood, make sure you buy it from a reputable supplier – young or badly-seasoned wood will only lead to tears! You will encounter a variety of cuts, all of which will have been used by cabinet makers in the past. Try to match the original wood as closely as possible, studying unfinished sections of timber for clues about the original cut. Even specialist suppliers will not custom cut to suit the restorer's requirements. However, you will usually be allowed to choose from the pile. Be warned: finding the right piece can take time and everyone's patience. Where a good match is essential (and this applies particularly to veneer, see pages 16–17), it will help to go armed with a piece of the original or a good photograph.

Most suppliers can provide a limited cutting service: the piece you need should be cut at least two weeks before

On this cross-section cut from a oak each ring represents a year of growth; on tropical trees such as mahogany this is not so clearly discernible. The fully developed centre of the tree is known as the heartwood, and the still developing, soft, outermost wood is called the sapwood. In many trees the latter is discarded.

❶ RIFT SAWING
Wood is split into cake-like slices and then squared up. Frequently used in early furniture, the cut affords stability and interesting graining. The wastage involved means that this is now a rare cut.

❷ QUARTER SAWN AND SQUARED
The tree is quartered, squared and sawn into baulks that can warp off true, losing their right angles.

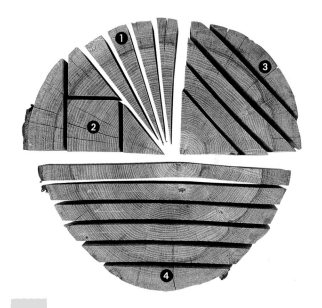

❸ TANGENTIAL SAWING
Planks produced by this method are decoratively marked with annular rings, but they have less stability and tend to warp away from the heartwood.

❹ PLAIN SAWING
This cut creates rather dull figuring and instability – only the centre board is unlikely to warp. The commonest method today, it is very economical.

making the repair. Bear in mind that regular restorers lay down wood rather like wine – as far ahead as possible. If you have several planks, stack them with small wood slivers between each one to allow air to circulate and remember to hand-plane the surface before use, however smooth (and time-saving) the supplier's initial electrical planing might be.

As a beginner, there is no need to despair of restoration that requires turned replacement parts. You may not have a lathe, but a specialist wood turner will do the job for you. Check local trade directories or ask your wood merchant for a recommendation. Turning is a fascinating craft and with luck you will be able to watch work in progress.

BUYING WOOD VENEERS

Increasingly, veneers can be bought through mail-order, a useful service but not always appropriate for restoration work, which often requires careful matching to existing veneers. A trip to a veneer supplier is a real treat: while you check for colour and figuring you'll see a sumptuous array of wood you never knew existed. Do not expect to be sold perfectly trimmed and squared pieces – burrs, for instance, whose every centimetre is precious, are left in their initial irregular shapes to avoid any wastage. It is good practice to stick lengths of veneer tape across the ends of veneers – however uneven – to prevent splitting.

Be prepared, also, to accept substitute veneers. For a recent repair on a French Empire bureau veneered in glorious Cuban mahogany, now unobtainable, we had to settle for an 'Indian' mahogany. (The seeds of this particular species had come from Cuba in the 19th century.)

Antique, hand-sawn veneers are considerably thicker (3mm) than the machine-cut veneers produced since the mid-19th century. They have, indeed, become progressively thinner and most are now approx. 0.8mm thick. Although suppliers usually stock a limited range of thicker veneers, you may have to glue several layers of thin veneer together and, once the glue has set, plane the bottom layer so that the laminate matches the original veneer.

Opposite are some of the decorative cuts most commonly used to produce the veneer encountered in restoration work. One of the more unusual cuts (not illustrated here) is the cross-section, which produced the 17th- and 18th-century oyster veneer. Transverse slices were cut across narrow-diameter woods such as laburnum or olive, creating a concentric grain pattern which resembled an oyster shell.

❶ BUTT CUT
Some of the most attractive wild-grain figuring is taken from the section of trunk just above the roots. Here fibres are distorted by changes in growth direction or by compression. When cut for veneer, the wood can be used to create interesting effects, often being laid to create patterns, such as star bursts. Butts are difficult to machine cut.

❷ FLAME OR CROTCH CUT
Taken at the point where the main trunk divides into two branches, the veneer produced has a distinctive figuring which resembles a flame or feathered plume. The effect was very highly prized in the early 19th century, when mahogany flame was used to enhance flat expanses of Empire-style furniture. A fragile veneer, this one requires careful handling.

❸ BURL OR BURR CUT
These wart-like protrusions appear on tree trunks as a reaction to insects or disease and are formed by the haphazard growth of stunted shoots. When sliced for veneer, the beautiful figuring appears as a swirling group of tiny knot formations. Rare and brittle, burls are dried with a higher moisture content than normal, making them less likely to crack or break.

HOW WOOD BEHAVES

Always bear in mind the 'living' qualities of wood. However stabilized by the seasoning process or the passing of years, it remains sensitive to temperature and humidity changes. Think of it as a sponge: in damp conditions it absorbs water from the air and expands; in dry conditions it loses moisture and shrinks. Sadly, the modern-day comfort of central heating has inflicted enormous damage upon much fine furniture, causing it to split and warp or cracking painted and gilded surfaces. If you must live in a hot-house, invest in a humidifier and hang specifically-designed water containers over radiators – your skin will reap the benefits too!

COMMON WOODS

WOOD	DESCRIPTION
1 Ash *Fraxinus excelsior*	• Colour varies from milky white to fawn brown.
2 Beech *Fagus sylvatica*	• Yellowy-brown in colour. • When steamed, can turn pinkish. • Flecked figuring.
3 Birch *Betula* species	• Soft brown colour. • Can be nicely figured with a wavy grain. When steamed, becomes highly flexible. • Close-grained wood.
4 Cherry *Prunus* species	• Fine example of the fruitwood family. • Colour varies from yellowy cream to dark reddish tan. • Fine textured, straight grained.
5 Cuban Mahogany *Swietenia mahogani*	• Dark, ruddy brown, often cross grained. • Highly figured. • White deposit in the grain (in late 19th century the grain of cheaper mahoganies was filled with plaster of Paris to imitate this feature).
6 Honduras Mahogany *Swietenia macrophylla*	• Orange-brown in colour. • Highly figured or string grained. • Fine texture.
7 African (or pseudo) Mahogany *Khaya ivoirensis*	• Lighter, less attractively marked than true mahogany. Pinkish tinge in natural state. • Open-pored grain.
8 Oak *Quercus* species	• Colour can vary from yellow-brown to mid-brown. • Open-pored grain.

HOW/WHEN USED	ADVANTAGES	DISADVANTAGES
• Used in North America for both rustic and more sophisticated furniture. • Often used for tool handles and also for Windsor chairs.	• Tough and flexible – suitable for turned pieces. • Bends and works well. • Polishes up to a good sheen.	• Decays in damp conditions. • Subject to infestation.
• Used mostly for carcase work and structural repairs. • Used extensively since 18th century for chair frames, veneered with more attractive woods or painted.	• Hard wood – very suitable for turned pieces. • Good surface for paint.	• Decays in damp conditions. • Liable to infestation. • Heavy.
• Birch-rod dowelling was used from late 19th century as a cheap replacement for the mortise and tenon joint. • Also used for bentwood furniture (including Thonet designs) and for modern plywood.	• Hard wood but relatively easy to work. • When polished, can imitate cherry and maple.	• Relatively heavy.
• Used for solid structures, also for decorative inlay and turned legs. • Widely used in continental Europe for furniture making in 18th and 19th centuries. Also in North America, where is known as American Mahogany.	• Strong wood but works well. • Good lustre when polished. • Does not warp or shrink. • Stains well. • Can resemble the more expensive, less attainable Honduras Mahogany.	• Lacks 'character'.
• Cabinet timber *par excellence*, in use from c. 1750, both for veneer and solid structures.	• Resists warping, decay and infestation. • Unites extremely well with glue. • Polishes well. • Colour improves with age.	• Difficult to find. • Difficult to match for restoration. • Brittle to work.
• In use from late 18th century onwards, both for veneer and solid structures. • Used in restoration – when it can be found – to replace Cuban Mahogany. • Can be darkened with bichromate of potash.	• Lighter, softer wood – easy to work. • Seasons well, with no tendency to crack or twist. • Resists warping, decay and infestation. • Unites well with glue. • Polishes well.	• Easily dented and scratched.
• Used since 1870s to replace decreasing supplies of true mahogany. • Cuts into very fine veneer so large areas can be covered cheaply: much used for reproduction and mass-produced furniture, for veneer and carcase work.	• Much easier to find and less expensive than true mahogany.	• Grain usually needs filling before polishing. See Cuban Mahogany for traditional solution; good-quality proprietary fillers available but not recommended for restoration work because tend to obscure the grain
• Extensively used for centuries, both for carcase work and solid country furniture and cabinet making. • 'Revived' in 1890s by the Arts and Crafts movement. • Popular with fakers.	• Strong, reliable and durable – few other woods resist so well the test of time. • Recommended for invisible repairs. • Stains well. • Beautiful finish can be achieved with beeswax polish.	• Difficult to work. • Stains black when iron left on it. • Needs long seasoning. • Subject to infestation. • Shrinkage can warp and twist. • Subject to infestation.

WOOD	DESCRIPTION
9 European Walnut *Juglans regia*	• Varies from light to dark greyish-brown. • Exquisite, unique figurings.
10 American Walnut *Juglans nigra*	• Darker than European Walnut, although in early American furniture can be light or greyish brown, similar to European Walnut. • Attractive figuring.
11 Burl Walnut	• A 'curly' graining with pin-head eyes, caused (like all burls) by an anomaly – viral or otherwise. • Found chiefly in European Walnut, less in American.
12 Cedar *Cedrus* species	• Pale orange colour. • Striped figuring. • Coarse grained. • Easily distinguished by its distinctive smell.
13 Pine *Pinus* species	• Colour varies from almost white to orangey-brown.
14 Macassar *Macassar* species	• Blackish or dark brown, pronounced streaks in grey, yellowish or red tones. • Can look spectacular when sawn tangentially (see page 15). • Dense texture.
15 Rosewood *Dalbergia nigra* (Brazilian) *Dalbergia latifolia* (S.E. Asia)	• Can vary from pale brown with black streaks (Brazilian variety) to tawny brown with purplish stripes (tulipwood). • Coarse, open grain and oily texture.
16 Satinwood *Fagara flava*	• Attractive golden colour. • Close grained. • Unique fine texture. • High oil content and curious smell of coconut when worked.

HOW/WHEN USED	ADVANTAGES	DISADVANTAGES
• One of the finest of the cabinet woods. Widely used since 16th century, much favoured in decorative pieces. • Largely forsaken in metropolitan cabinet work when mahogany came into use. • Beautiful effects obtained in veneering.	• Medium-hard wood but easy to work. • Polishes very well: beeswax for earlier pieces, French polish for later pieces.	• Now in short supply: for repairs try to find old wood. • Expensive.
• Supplied the first English colonists with material for their bows. Later recognized as the finest wood of the North American forests and can be found in pieces made in the original 13 states. Use of walnut in America was never entirely dropped in favour of mahogany.	• More resistant to infestation, particularly from the furniture beetle, than European Walnut. • Medium-hard wood, highly satisfactory for chair and cabinet making. • Polishes well.	• More difficult to work than European Walnut. • Expensive.
• Due to rarity, used principally for veneering. • Often seen on the dashboard of prestigious British cars or carved into pipe bowls.	• Highly prized, like all burls, particularly decorative and attractive.	• Difficult to apply as veneer. • Like all highly figured woods, difficult to match in restoration: the restorer can resort to *faux bois*.
• Used mainly for drawer linings, panelling and structural work. Also to line wardrobes and make blanket boxes. • To seal in the natural oils or enhance the grain, use a shellac finish.	• Easy to work. • Aromatic oils in wood repel all insects – especially moths.	• Bruises easily.
• Used plain and waxed for country furniture or painted, veneered or lacquered. Also used for carcase work. • Frequently given a *faux-bois* finish in 19th century.	• Soft, light wood – cheap and easy to work.	• Easily scratched. • Liable to warp. • Subject to knots and splits – can leak resin.
• Used as veneer in cabinet making – an alternative to ebony. • Beloved of French *ébénistes* during the Art Deco period.	• Magnificent, highly unusual and decorative exotic wood.	• Rare and expensive. • Relatively heavy.
• Used extensively in Europe for veneering during 18th century and in North America from Empire period onwards. • When rejoining rosewood, degrease the surface with carbon tetrachloride. • Be careful if stripping: darker wood lies just under the surface.	• Hard, exotic, highly decorative.	• Difficult to work. • Splinters easily. • Difficult to glue. • Veneer tends to crack easily.
• Used for veneer and often inlaid with dark woods, such as ebony. • Favoured by Chippendale, Hepplewhite and Phyfe.	• Decorative wood. • Mellows well with age.	• Rare and expensive. • Glues badly due to high oil content. • When polished with beeswax, tends to lose its colour. • Inflammable (due to oil content).

BEFORE YOU BEGIN

Armed with an awareness of how wood behaves, you can now turn to the practicalities of restoration. Start with a relatively simple and inexpensive piece – the bedside cabinet pictured below would be an ideal subject to practise on. You will simplify your work and avoid mistakes if you follow a logical, step-by-step procedure such as that set out opposite, bearing in mind that furniture, and its problems, can vary enormously and that inevitably you may need to leave out or reschedule some of the steps we propose, particularly if dealing with 'modern classics'.

We found this piece in the 'good for firewood' corner of a Swiss charity shop. The surface resembled grained pine, but when a wet fingertip was run over it we saw at once the beauty of burr walnut.

Remember: there are two golden rules for successful restoration work. First: take your time. Most old furniture was carefully thought out in terms of design and construction and making it was a lengthy process by today's standards. Accordingly, your work should not be hurried. Rushed or misinformed restoration is one of the principal causes of damaged furniture. Second: never forget that your aim is to restore, not to transform or renew. Any work you carry out should be, as far as is possible, *reversible*. This is an essential precept and, you will also find, a *leitmotiv* throughout this book.

Cracked and warped solid walnut top
(CONSOLIDATION)

Crack in pine carcase
(CONSOLIDATION)

**Drawer collapsed
when prized free**
(CONSOLIDATION)

Knobs need replacing

Loose burr veneer
(VENEER REPAIRS)

**Burr walnut veneer
bloomed and crazed**
(SURFACE REPAIRS)

Woodworm
(INFESTATION)

Missing corner
(PAINTED WASHSTAND,
p.145, Repairs, step 3)

Pivot hinge failure
(METAL FITTINGS)

ORGANIZING YOUR RESTORATION PROJECT

Take a 'before' photo – once the piece is transformed, you'll regret not having a record of the ugly duckling. Check for INFESTATION (see page 36) and treat if necessary, both before carcase restoration and after surface repairs. To identify the exact nature of a finish, make a test strip (see page 38) on an inconspicuous area. CLEANING (see page 38) comes next: this will help you to assess the extent of damage and establish the type of wood you are dealing with. Make a job list of possible repairs set out in logical order. Check that your tools and materials are assembled and conform to safety procedures (see page 29). Remove any detachable parts, such as drawers or doors, which could hinder repairs, and put any small, loose objects – metal fittings, stray screws, chipped-off veneer – into transparent plastic wallets for safe-keeping. Carefully remove and store worn-out UPHOLSTERY (see page 72): this is a job to return to once any repairs and refinishing have been carried out. If STRIPPING (see page 39) cannot be avoided, this is usually the appropriate time.

Our beechwood replacement knobs were found in an old-fashioned ironmonger's shop. We stained them black, using nitro stain (see page 112), followed by a coat of shellac (see page 98, Shellac as Varnish). They looked suitably authentic on this 1900s piece.

You may need to DISMANTLE the piece (see page 43) to facilitate repairs – proceed with great caution, marking all the parts with a Chinagraph to simplify re-assembly. Have ready plenty of protection for fragile parts, such as marble tops or mirrors. A stock of old blankets and newspapers is useful here. When carrying out CONSOLIDATION (see page 43), remember that one of the principles of restoration is to replace as little as possible. Antique furniture which loses more than 20 per cent of its original structure plummets in value. Make a 'dry run' for correct fit before re-assembly, especially if this involves GLUING (see page 45) and CLAMPING (see page 47).

Once the piece is stable, effect UPHOLSTERY (see page 72), SURFACE (see page 82) and VENEER REPAIRS (see page 88) and attend to METAL FITTINGS (see page 67). This is also the time to STAIN (see page 112), before you restore or apply appropriate FINISHES (pages 94–111 and 116–123).

TOOLS AND MATERIALS

Although a purpose-built shed is the ideal work space, a garage or spare room can prove adequate given the right preparation. Essentials include ventilation, a good light source (ideally both natural and artificial) and heating, particularly if gluing or polishing. An adjustable workbench provides a stable surface for clamping work when drilling or cutting; if short of space, choose one that can be folded down.

Aspiring restorers, faced with a huge shopping list of tools and materials, can be easily discouraged by the choice and financial outlay involved. Fear not! Assuming you already have a basic household DIY kit, you will find in this section a useful guide to the extra purchases you need to make to accomplish a wide variety of restoration work.

A electric drill and jigsaw are an advantage but for most restoration work the emphasis is on hand tools. Indeed, in many instances hand-work is the only means of doing a job. To build up an inexpensive but good-quality tool collection (very cheap tools are a false economy) investigate the small ads. in specialist papers and magazines and go to boot sales. But remember: most new tools come with comprehensive safety instructions and this will not always be the case with second-hand tools so take the time to learn how to use them correctly. A wood-working manual would be a wise investment for beginners.

MEASURING AND MARKING

Professional restorers will often rely on their 'eye' when assessing size but the amateur would be well advised to take accurate measurements: have a locking tape measure and a stainless steel rule always at the ready. (The rule can also be used as a guide and support when cutting with a craft knife.) On antique pieces do not be surprised to find slight differences on seemingly identical components, such as chair legs or the two halves of a table.

Cabinet makers often use a craft knife (see page 27) to mark and score wood which needs to be cut, ensuring a clean, straight line. It is also worth remembering to cut new work slightly oversize – if necessary, you can trim it down but never up!

ACCURACY
From the top
A sliding bevel, marking gauge and try square – all musts for precise cutting jobs, such as making new joints. Additional aids might include a spirit level to ensure perfect horizontals and Chinagraph pencils for marking.

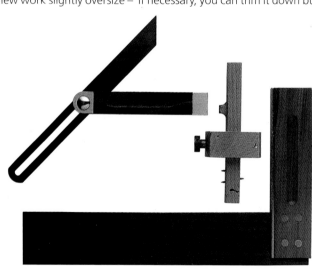

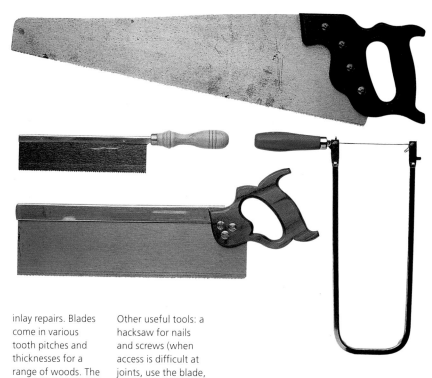

SAWS
From the top
The wood worker's cross-cut (or hand) saw is customary for general purposes. A gent's saw can be used for sawing dovetail joints or other fine cuts: the name may derive from the fact that, pre 20th-century, wood-working was a 'gentleman's' hobby. The tenon saw is restoration's standard saw. Designed for tenon joints, it cuts other joints accurately and works well across the grain. Check that the 'spine' is heavy – weight makes for easier cutting. If you are not using an electric jigsaw, a fretsaw is essential for shaped or curved work, such as veneer for inlay repairs. Blades come in various tooth pitches and thicknesses for a range of woods. The finer blades break easily: practise on waste veneer first, moving the veneer into the blade.

Other useful tools: a hacksaw for nails and screws (when access is difficult at joints, use the blade, wrapping one end with masking tape), large and small craft knives (see page 27) and stout scissors.

CHISELS AND GOUGES
From the left
A basic kit should include: a mortise chisel (1–2), its handle designed to be hit with a mallet and used to chop out mortise joints; a paring chisel (3–4) with bevelled edges for fine paring and fitting around joints, used alone or very lightly tapped with a mallet, and a firmer chisel (5–6), a stronger, general-purpose tool. For carving small details, you can improvise with a craft knife, a rasp (7) and simple gouges. Gouges resemble curved chisels and fall into into two groups: firmers (8–9, 11), which are bevelled on the outside for cutting concave shapes, and parers (10, 12), bevelled on the inside for convex shapes.

USING CHISELS AND GOUGES

• Mark out the area you wish to cut and start cutting within the marked area, paring back carefully towards the marked line.

• Keep good-quality chisels for cutting. Use another set for dismantling and cleaning up.

• Sharpen and hone chisels regularly, using an oil stone. A blunt chisel is dangerous.

PLANES

From the top
Hand planes are a major feature in the restorer's tool chest. The jack plane, with its long sole, is useful for removing really rough surfaces before using a smoothing plane. The small, low-angled block-plane is used for awkward end grain and for touching-up work. It is particularly suited to the brittle woods often found in restoration. The smoothing plane is vital for smoothing along the grain. Spokeshaves are useful for curved surfaces. Metal ones with adjustable cutters are best. Planes are available in wood or metal: wooden tools have a highly satisfying 'feel' but are now harder to find.

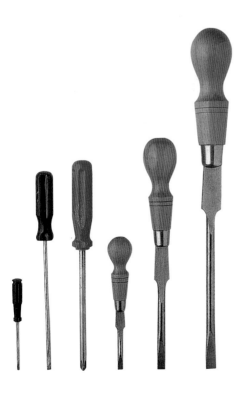

SCREWDRIVERS

From the left
An electrician's slot-head, a large slot-head, a Philips cross-head and three traditional cabinet maker's screwdrivers – all used for a variety of our projects. The flat section at the top of the cabinet maker's screwdriver is designed to allow for extra leverage. It is the width of the slot in the screw-head that determines the size of the screwdriver. An ill-fitting tool will mangle the screw. Using the right screwdriver is vital when working on antiques or 'modern classics' because original screws should be kept whenever possible. We check regularly that the tips are clean and square and, when dealing with finer antique screws, we sharpen the screwdriver slightly with an oilstone. Blunt and battered screwdrivers are only good for opening paint tins! Nails can be much tougher to remove than screws and a good pair of pincers is essential.

EQUIPMENT FOR VENEERING

Veneering is a specialized craft and requires a few specific tools: don't rush to buy them until you have mastered some of the basics of furniture restoration. However, there is one you are likely to have to hand: a craft knife, with replaceable blades, is useful for cutting veneer. The blades should be extremely thin along the cutting edge and sharply pointed to enable the knife to get into small, tight areas. Hold the knife at a 30° angle to the veneer when cutting. Use an oilstone to keep the blades sharpened and choose the surface you cut on with care – a hard surface will dull your blade and a soft one will make for fuzzy edges on the veneer. Special cutting mats are good but expensive: you can use a plywood offcut or thick cardboard instead. An old domestic electric (non-steam) iron will also be necessary – do not expect to use it again for ironing clothes!

SPECIAL TOOLS
From top left
Veneer tape is a special gummed paper tape used for maintaining joins between veneer pieces. Moisten it slightly to remove. A wooden toothing plane has an almost vertical blade with a serrated edge which both evens out irregularities and leaves tiny marks on the groundwork to 'key' it. Use as if you were scouring a table top. New planes are hard to find, but they are still available second-hand. An old tenon saw is a possible, if poor, substitute. A veneer saw is useful for cutting thin veneers. Its curved blade ensures a clean, straight cut. Use a batten as a guide For more complex angles and curves use a fretsaw. The veneer hammer is not a hammer at all, but simply a wooden holder with a metal strip set into its head. It is used to squeeze out both air and surplus glue for firm contact with the groundwork. Last, a non-specialist tool: the invaluable craft knife.

CLAMPING

Much of your work in restoration will involve gluing surfaces or parts together, and clamps are essential for squeezing out excess glue and ensuring firm, even contact (see page 47). They also provide stability for cutting jobs. However, care must be taken not to fracture the fibres of your wood surfaces or damage finishes. Always slip protective plywood offcuts between the jaws and the surface, and when clamping square frames small, L-shaped moulding pieces (available from DIY centres) are ideal for protecting corners. Although some clamps are inexpensive, you can improvise your own with lengths of cord wrapped around the object and tightened with a length of dowel, or even use rubber bands and clothes pegs. We also find jubilee (or hose) clamps useful for an even pressure around cylindrical surfaces such as turned legs, where other clamps would slip off (see page 52).

SIMPLE CLAMPS
From the left
You can never have too many G-clamps. Use them to hold work steady when cutting, as well as when gluing. Aim for as wide a range of sizes as possible. Tightened with a hand-screw, they can exert a lot of pressure. The deep-throat type (top left) is great for awkward shapes. Webbing clamps are also excellent, both for curved or unwieldy shapes and for applying pressure from all angles.

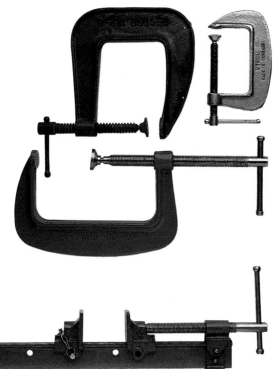

SASH AND SPEED CLAMPS
From the left
You need at least two sash clamps for tightening up joints and general carcase repairs, where a controlled pressure is required. Used in tandem for panel work, the bars prevent the wood from buckling. The T-bar sash type (above) is even better: it will not bend and is useful for heavy work. Lightweight speed clamps are more versatile, being suitable for work where support bars are not necessary. They come with protective jaw pads and can be reversed for dismantling pieces (see page 45).

SAFETY PRECAUTIONS

A good workshop is a well-maintained one. Make it a rule to keep your work space clean and tidy – a littered workbench and congested floor area will not only hinder the progress of your work but are also safety hazards. Be aware that many of the materials used in restoration are potentially dangerous – poisonous, flammable or corrosive – and take the necessary precautions. Remember: common sense is the best protection.

HANDLING HAZARDOUS MATERIALS

- Keep materials in a locked, fireproof cabinet and label containers clearly.
- Never store material in empty food or freezer containers.
- Do not be tempted to throw materials down the drain – check with local authorities to find out what method of disposal they recommend.
- Never leave used rags or bits of wirewool lying around – they present a fire hazard.
- Install a suitable fire extinguisher, fire blanket and sand-filled bucket in the workshop.

PROTECTION
From top left
Protective clothing should always include a heavy-duty apron or overalls. Wear approved-standard goggles to protect your eyes from splashes and irritation from chemicals or dust. A mask prevents dust inhalation and can filter fumes. Check its recommended uses; some filters are designed to catch coarse dust particles only. A selection of gloves is important: spirit-resistant vinyl gloves for most work, heavy-duty elbow-length industrial gloves for stripping, and cotton gloves when working with abrasives or for handling small gilding jobs. Ear protectors may sometimes be necessary: use either ear muffs or ear plugs. Don't forget to protect the work space too – with newspaper.

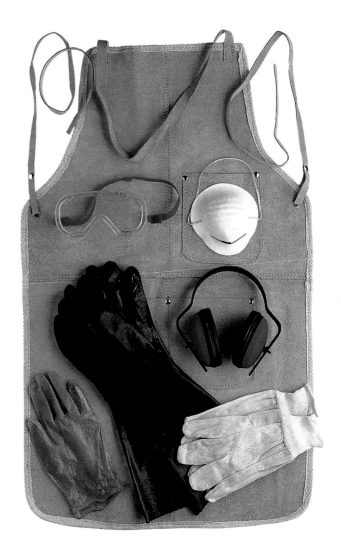

SYRINGES AND NEEDLES

We buy veterinary syringes in 10-packs from specialist suppliers (see page 172). For injecting insecticide (see page 36) and hot pearl glue (see page 47), we always use a large (50ml) syringe. Needles come in a variety of terrifying sizes. The two we find most useful are: 1.2mm x 40mm and 1.65mm x 40mm (imperial: 18 gauge x 1½in and 16 gauge x 1½in). You'll probably have to buy in bulk (relatively cheaply) – unless your local vet knows you well.

BRUSHES AND COLOUR

No, old furniture does not just come in shades of brown! You will certainly find coloured, painted pieces that need their paintwork restored or replaced and for this you should make sure that you use the correct type of paint and colours that remain true to the original spirit. Colour preferences have changed quite radically over the centuries and an 18th-century palette is very different from a 20th-century one. Paint consists of pigment ground into a medium. The medium binds the pigment together and can be either oil or water based or, in some cases, wax. Whiting can be added to gouache to increase opacity.

Brushes have a significant place in the furniture restorer's kit – you'll find you need a variety for specific applications and techniques. Each brush has different characteristics – derived from its size, form and the type of bristle or hair employed – and it is worth using the right brush for the particular job in hand. If you can, pay a little extra for the best quality: it does make for a finer finish and the brushes will last much longer, provided you clean them properly after use and hang them from a hook to dry. They will keep their shape much better than if stored flat.

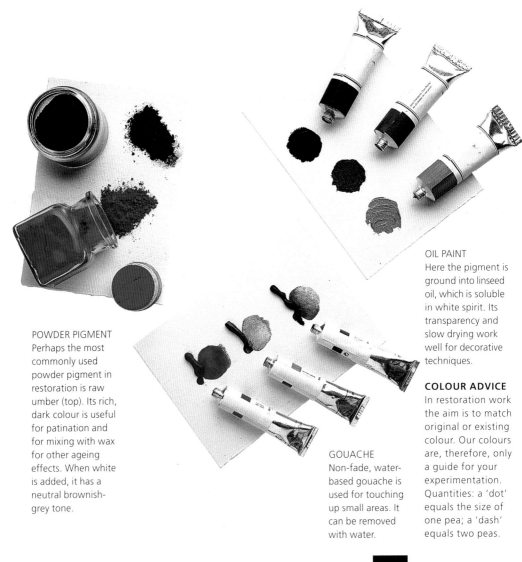

POWDER PIGMENT
Perhaps the most commonly used powder pigment in restoration is raw umber (top). Its rich, dark colour is useful for patination and for mixing with wax for other ageing effects. When white is added, it has a neutral brownish-grey tone.

GOUACHE
Non-fade, water-based gouache is used for touching up small areas. It can be removed with water.

OIL PAINT
Here the pigment is ground into linseed oil, which is soluble in white spirit. Its transparency and slow drying work well for decorative techniques.

COLOUR ADVICE
In restoration work the aim is to match original or existing colour. Our colours are, therefore, only a guide for your experimentation. Quantities: a 'dot' equals the size of one pea; a 'dash' equals two peas.

USEFUL BRUSHES
From the left
The hog-bristled varnish brush is a finer version of the household paint brush (next right). Being thinner, there is less risk of over-load, which means fewer drips. Despite its name, it is useful for fine layers of paint so keep a brush just for this. Never use your varnish brush for paint or vice versa, unless you want to ruin clear surfaces. The ubiquitous household paint brush is also made from hog's bristle; a general-purpose brush, we use the 25mm size most frequently. The gesso brush is 'bridled' with string to keep its hairs stiff and straight; move the bridle up as the hairs on the tip become worn. A small, coarse-haired glue brush will suit for most restoration jobs, but use a big one for laying large sections of veneer. Another adjustable brush, its bridle is made from wire.

DECORATION
From the left
A flogging brush can be used for graining effects. Traditionally of horse hair, its fibres are excellent for the tapping motion of 'flogging' (see page 117). A medium, round sable brush is expensive but very special! Its flexibility is unmatched and, due to the elliptical shape of sable hairs, it will always retain its shape and more importantly its point. Use with water- or oil-based paint: it's a precision tool for marbling, graining and touching up small details. The spalter, with its very thin, fine bristles, is used for graining and touching in semi-transparent washes. A white-bristled dusting brush, designed to dust off sanded surfaces before painting, makes a good blender on oil-based decorative finishes.

ABRASIVES
A wire brush (top) can be used to smooth most rough surfaces or to strip carved mouldings. Substitute a bronze brush (right) when dealing with oak – the iron in wire will discolour this highly tannic wood.

FINISHING

Abrasives are usually needed in the finishing stages of restoration or for preparation. They should always be chosen with care and used with restraint since their misuse can ruin a patina or remove the slightly uneven surface texture which often gives old furniture its special charm. Glass or sand papers are graded by grit size. The lower the number, the coarser the grade. Unfortunately, there is no absolute universal standard and even the colours differ. Our equipment lists are a guide to the appropriate grades for a variety of common restoration jobs. When checking progress while using abrasives, remember that your fingertips can often tell you just as much as your eyes.

Even the most beautiful woods sometimes need a little outside help from enhancers such as polishes and waxes. There is a vast choice out there but *your* choice will be dictated by the finish you intend to restore – in no time you will build up a collection of little pots and potions to suit a whole variety of tasks. If in doubt when matching the colour of shellac or wax sticks to your wood, opt for the darker shade.

PAPER ABRASIVES
From the left
Wet and dry paper (1) lubricated with water is a good way to cut back oil-based paints and varnishes. Two grades of aluminium oxide paper: use a coarse one (3) for preparation and a finer variety (2) between finishing coats. Garnet paper (4) is a good-quality sandpaper for soft and hard wood. Two grades of silicone-carbide paper (5–6): the finer (6) is for superfine finishes, as in French polishing – powder plugs the gaps between the grit to prevent clogging and cut scratching.

WIRE & SYNTHETIC ABRASIVES
From top left
Stainless-steel pan scourers can be useful for stripping jobs, but wirewool is really the restorer's favourite. It is flexible so easier to control than paper, and it clogs less. Don't tear it: cut it. Sold in rolls, it is graded, the finest just glossing the surface. Synthetic abrasives (also graded) can be used for stripping, especially oak.

SANDING TO FINISH

- For new wood and oak, choose 120-grade sandpaper. For old wood and veneer, choose 180-grade sandpaper.

- Use the lightest possible touch – your aim is to unify the surface, not to cut it. When working with new veneer, simply get rid of the 'fluff'.

- Dust with a just damp rag, leaving no moisture on the surface.

PROPRIETARY SHELLAC POLISHES

TYPE	DESCRIPTION	USE
French (or brown polish) **Standard**	Mid brown	Mostly for mahogany, but its dark colour obscures the grain of the wood. Not recommended for restoration work.
Garnet	Dark reddish-brown	For oak and mahogany. Although widely recommended for restoration work and replacement parts, it also tends to obscure the grain and can make lighter woods too dark.
Button	Golden brown. Made from shellac 'buttons'. Hard finish.	For lighter woods but to be used with discretion. Can look unpleasantly orange.
White	Milky white. Made from bleached shellac. Slow drying	For light woods, such as sycamore and ash. Has the same darkening effect as water.
Transparent (or clear)	Colourless and very hard. Made from bleached and de-waxed shellac	Ideal for woods where no colour change is required. Recommended for restoration work. For replacement parts, stain new wood to match and then apply the polish.

SHELLAC

A centuries-old, favourite finishing material, used as varnish or (later) as the main ingredient in French polish, shellac originates from India. It is made from a secretion of the female lac beetle (centre right). This is then melted, refined, crushed (centre), and sold either in raw flakes (see plates) or, as we recommend, dissolved in alcohol (see pots). The proportion of shellac to alcohol is known as the 'cut'. Shellac sticks (centre, far right) are a concentrated form of shellac and are sold in a variety of 'woody' colours. They are used to fill in cracks and holes and are melted with a soldering iron.

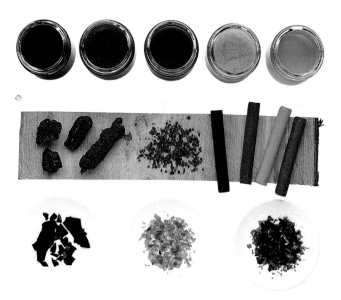

BEESWAX

Pure beeswax from the honeycomb is the main ingredient of good polish. Although you can make your own polishes by heating wax and turpentine, this can be highly flammable and we recommend good-quality proprietary beeswax. Carnauba wax, which comes from the Brazilian wax palm, is added sometimes to produce a harder wax particularly suitable for turned woods. Wax sticks (left) are useful for minor repairs such as filling small holes but cannot be used under modern finishes.

OTHER MATERIALS

UPHOLSTERY

In past centuries, the upholsterer was often considered more important than his fellow craftsman, the cabinet maker. He was responsible not just for seat furniture but all soft furnishings, such as wall and bed hangings. He had a great influence upon the arrangement of the room and in many ways anticipated today's interior decorator. It is a great advantage to acquire a few simple upholstery skills. Interesting old chairs and sofas really drop in price when they need re-upholstering and this is one area where bargains can still be had. Most beginners start with the basic essentials and gradually build up their tool kit as they tackle more ambitious work. The tools discussed here make a good starting point. Be sure you have a clean, light space in which to work. A large table top is suitable for some work but trestles adapted to support the work at a comfortable height are even better

GILDING

Gilding also has a singular, special place in restoration – its own particular mystique. The tools themselves are specialized and should be kept apart from all other workshop tools. We keep ours wrapped in protective pouches placed in a polished box made just for this purpose. There's always a pleasurable little thrill when we open that box.

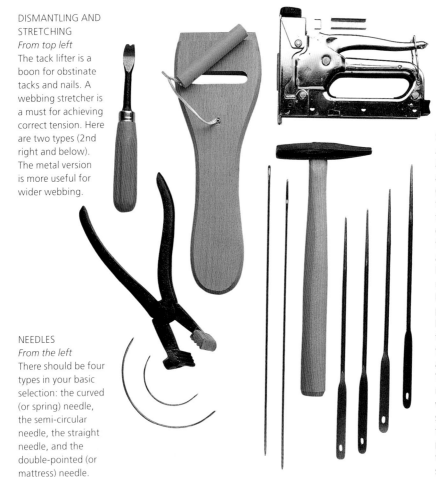

DISMANTLING AND STRETCHING
From top left
The tack lifter is a boon for obstinate tacks and nails. A webbing stretcher is a must for achieving correct tension. Here are two types (2nd right and below). The metal version is more useful for wider webbing.

NEEDLES
From the left
There should be four types in your basic selection: the curved (or spring) needle, the semi-circular needle, the straight needle, and the double-pointed (or mattress) needle.

SECURING AND ADJUSTING
From the top
A hand-held staple gun may not be traditional but it is a tremendous help, causing less damage than rows of tacks. An upholstery hammer with a magnetic head will let you pick up and position tacks, leaving one hand free to manipulate fabric. Regulators are indispensable. They are used mainly to distribute various layers of stuffing evenly over the seat, and can be pushed through fabrics. The medium size is most useful.

HANDLING LEAF
From the left
The gilder's cushion, a padded board covered with calf-skin or chamois, is used when cutting loose leaf. Clean by rubbing with rouged tissues from a used book of leaves. The folding screen wards off draughts. A gilder's tip will pick up gold leaf. Made from squirrel hair, it comes in three widths to suit leaf size: medium is the best all-rounder.

Store between stiff card. The gilder's knife cuts the gold but not the cushion. Check the blade for irregularities and hone carefully as needed. We like this small, fine French version. Gilder's mops are made from dark squirrel hair or soft, white hog's hair (known as camel mops). Manipulate and fix leaf with the first. Apply size/bole, gilding water and shellac with the second.

POLISHING
Below
The burnishing tool used on loose leaf is usually made from agate. Store in a soft cloth roll to avoid scratches. Regular gilders will need a large and a small burnisher. For minor gilding work, a small one is enough.

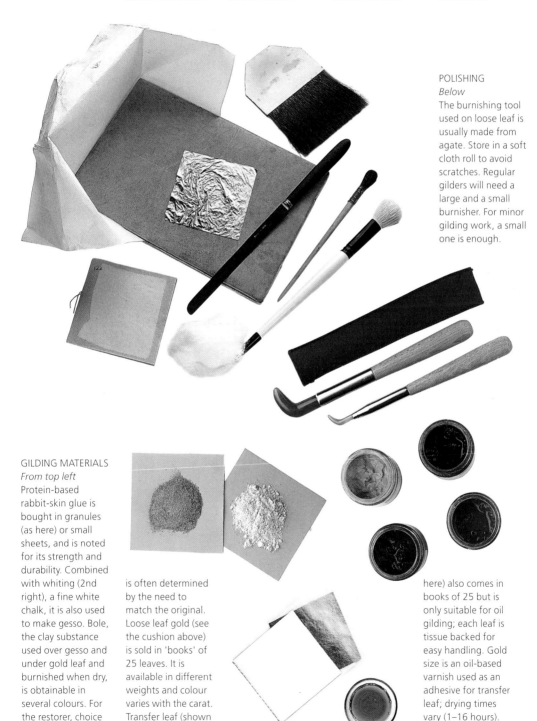

GILDING MATERIALS
From top left
Protein-based rabbit-skin glue is bought in granules (as here) or small sheets, and is noted for its strength and durability. Combined with whiting (2nd right), a fine white chalk, it is also used to make gesso. Bole, the clay substance used over gesso and under gold leaf and burnished when dry, is obtainable in several colours. For the restorer, choice is often determined by the need to match the original. Loose leaf gold (see the cushion above) is sold in 'books' of 25 leaves. It is available in different weights and colour varies with the carat. Transfer leaf (shown here) also comes in books of 25 but is only suitable for oil gilding; each leaf is tissue backed for easy handling. Gold size is an oil-based varnish used as an adhesive for transfer leaf; drying times vary (1–16 hours).

INFESTATION AND ROT

If you see worm holes on furniture, make this simple test: stand the piece on newspaper for a week, sharply tapping the affected area every day. Small piles of sawdust known as 'frass' indicate an active presence and you should act fast since beetles can spread with alarming rapidity. Never put newly-acquired pieces into furnished rooms until treatment has been carried out. Rot is a less prevalent problem for furniture, except in humid, tropical climates or when stored in damp conditions. Certain woods, such as beech and pine, are more prone than others.

TREATING WOODWORM

The voracious furniture beetle (*Anobium punctatum*) will attack both modern and antique furniture and is also partial to wooden floors, panelling and beams. The adult female lays her eggs in cracks and crevices – one reason why cabinet makers are taught to make surfaces and joint recesses as smooth as possible – and once hatched, the grubs burrow their way into the timber, creating a maze of galleries.

Initial preventive measures can be taken before cleaning. Repeat after a few weeks to be certain the insecticide has killed the larvae, adult insects and the eggs. If carrying out restoration, this second treatment should come before finishing, although quality insecticides will not harm finishes. The most effective time is early spring: adult females will not lay eggs on treated surfaces. Working outside or in a

well-ventilated space protected with plastic sheeting and newspaper and wearing spirit-resistant gloves, goggles and mask, try to blow as much frass as possible out of the holes. (We use a compressed-air camera cleaner.) Brush all surfaces with insecticide, following the manufacturer's instructions. Use a syringe (see page 29) to inject every hole with insecticide, making sure it penetrates completely. See also page 160 for a 'drip' system we recommend where extreme measures are needed.

TREATING OTHER PESTS

Death watch beetles
Make their presence known by a tapping sound during the mating season. Luckily they prefer structural housing timber. In the unlikely event of a problem, treat as for woodworm or send to a specialized fumigation centre.

Powder-post beetles
Prevalent in North America, treat as woodworm.

Termites (or white ants)
A problem in tropical countries. Tiled floors and specialized advice are a wise precaution if you have valuable furniture.

TREATING WOOD ROT

The often spectacular damage caused by central heating has already been discussed (see page 17). Here we look at the more insidious deterioration sustained by furniture kept in damp and airless conditions. First mould or mildew develops, creating dark stains or a furry aspect, and then the wood softens, crumbles and flakes. Moisture will also soften animal glues, loosen joints and lift veneer. (Animal glues are particularly attractive to fungus.) Chair and table feet, left standing for long periods on damp floors, will eventually rot away. Wooden picture frames, and their supporting cords, are also at risk when left hanging against humid walls.

Worm and rot have wreaked havoc on the beechwood mechanism of this gate-leg table. Unfortunately, it is now past repair and must be replaced (see page 56).

Furniture found in these conditions should be left to dry out very slowly and gently in a moderately warm, ventilated room – sudden changes of temperature will only cause more damage. Open any drawers or doors on the piece and leave for several weeks before assessing restoration. This will also give animal glue time to reconstitute itself (if it has not been destroyed by mould) and hopefully re-create bonds which may have softened. If necessary, use a proprietary treatment against rot or fungus.

REPAIRING DAMAGED FURNITURE

Worm or rot may have damaged the piece to such an extent that you have to consider two extreme measures.

Cutting out Removing and replacing the damaged part altogether is not a reversible process so we would only consider this method if the part is subject to stress, for example, a chair leg or a gate-leg table support.

Building up On small areas this can be done with sawdust and hot pearl glue (see page 45), mixed to a mastic consistency and packed into the holes and crevices. Try to use sawdust of the same type as the existing wood. When dry, sand with fine paper, stain if necessary and finish to match. You may also use a specialist two-part resin casting solution (reversible since it can be dissolved with acetone). This is liquid enough to be injected into the wood with a syringe (see page 47). Put masking tape around the repair so the resin does not leak out of any holes. Complete as above.

CLEANING AND STRIPPING

Removal of dirt, wax or silicone build-up clears the way for structural and other repairs and enables you to make informed decisions about how to treat the surface finish. Please note that over-zealous or inappropriate cleaning and stripping causes irretrievable damage: do not remove years of beautiful patina or fragile paintwork with vigorous rubbing or unsuitable products. A knowledge of finishes and the periods in which they were used is an invaluable guide to the restorer.

TEST STRIPPING TO IDENTIFY THE SURFACE

It is vital, before you begin cleaning, to analyze and identify all the surfaces and component parts of the piece. Metal inlay or gilding on a polished wood table, for example, will require very different treatments. Experienced restorers can recognize certain finishes at a glance but where they are hard to identify it is standard practice to run a simple test strip. We always recommend that beginners test strip on some inconspicuous part of the piece. It is an excellent way to identify a finish, and sometimes it will reveal an original finish beneath obscuring layers of polish, wax or pure grime. Rub the surface gently with clean cotton buds dipped in the substances listed below. Proceed in the sequence given, stopping as soon as you have the necessary information.

SUBSTANCE	ACTION
White spirit	Removes dirt and wax. If any colour is removed, surface is likely to be encaustic paint, coloured wax or oil gilding.
Methylated spirits	Removes French polish, shellac-based varnishes, modern acrylic-based paints and oil gilding. Caution: methylated spirits often contains water, which will remove water gilding.
Water	Removes water-based glue tempera, gouache, gesso and water gilding.
Solvent-based stripper	Removes oil paint, French polish, some acrylics, modern varnishes and lacquers, and oil gilding.

CLEANING WOOD FINISHES

For painted surfaces, we choose a solution of warm water and concentrated technical soap (see page 172). This additive-free product is also soluble in white spirit if your surface will be damaged by water. For French polished surfaces and wax or oil finishes, we use white spirit applied with rags or, if the dirt is deeply ingrained, fine to medium wirewool (grades 000–0). For removing traditional glues, use hot water, a household sponge and (if necessary) a blunted paint knife. The less complex the formula the less likelihood of unwelcome chemical reactions at the finishing stage.

Water is detrimental to wood and water-based paints so do not soak the surface when cleaning (using clean, lint-free rags or a sponge) and dry immediately with a clean rag. Once cleaned, you can decide if the finish is satisfactory, needs patching up or reviving, or, more drastically, stripping.

STRIPPING WOOD FINISHES

This is an irreversible process and should only be undertaken if the finish has deteriorated beyond repair, has been badly applied or is inappropriate for the style of the piece. Your watchwords should be extreme caution. Stripping methods to be routinely avoided range from laborious dry stripping, using a cabinet scraper and sandpaper (and sometimes removing patina into the bargain), to caustic dipping tanks (which can darken wood and wreak havoc with joints and glued surfaces). One of the rare occasions when we would recommend dry stripping is if you discover oil gilding under paint and wish to retain it.

Proprietary solvent-based paint strippers containing methylene chloride, applied with a brush and removed with wirewool, provide, we think, the least problematic solution (see page 40). They are easily controlled, do not raise the grain or darken wood, and can be used to remove all paints, cellulose-based finishes, modern varnishes and lacquers, French polish and any oil or wax not removed by cleaning. As the chart opposite makes clear, French polish can also be removed with methylated spirits – a method we use where careful partial stripping is required (see page 98, Repairs).

Stripping painted surfaces can be unpredictable, revealing poor or uneven colour tones, replacement parts and mis-matched woods and resembling nothing so much as a patchwork. If this is what confronts you and you do not plan to repaint, you might consider staining (see page 112).

SAFETY PRECAUTIONS

- Work outdoors in a well-ventilated area on several layers of newspaper.
- Remove metal fixtures and fittings unless sure that stripper will not discolour them.
- Wear protective clothing, industrial gloves and goggles.
- Follow the manufacturer's instructions: solvents are highly toxic.
- Do not smoke or drink alcohol.
- Wrap all waste in newspaper for prompt disposal. Never flush solvents down drains.

CLEANING AND STRIPPING

1 Decant the stripper into a clean metal or glass container and apply to small areas with a 25mm household paint brush. Spread thickly: thin, smooth coats will evaporate and reduce efficiency. Leave for 10–15 minutes.

2 Test with a blunted paint knife to see if the finish has softened and dissolved. When it has, remove the waste, working along the grain without damaging the wood. At least one more coat will be necessary.

3 Remove the last coat with medium or coarse wirewool (grade 0 for softwood, 2 for hardwood), following the grain. Rub gently on curves and mouldings. On difficult detail use a bronze brush and pads of hessian.

4 Neutralize any stripping residue on the surface by wiping down with a rag moistened with white spirit. This will not raise the grain and is generally sufficient treatment – unless the manufacturer states otherwise.

PREPARING FOR PAINTWORK

Any wooden surface that is to be painted needs some preparation: ideally a primer and undercoat should be applied before the top or finish coat in order to bond this final coat to the supporting surface. For restoration work, the approach should be one of reversibility – we recommend a gesso base (see page 100) and water-based colour, specifically artist's gouache. If planning to use an oil-based paint after gesso, it is best to seal the surface first with one coat of colourless proprietary shellac polish (see page 33), leaving it to dry for 24 hours. On brand-new surfaces – for example, before marbling or graining replacement parts, after dusting, fine sanding, and wiping down with dampened rags, apply a thin coat of good-quality, oil-based wood primer, followed by an oil-based undercoat, according to the manufacturer's recommended drying times.

CLEANING AND MAINTAINING OTHER SURFACES

CANE

Cleaning Use a mild solution of concentrated technical soap (see page 172) and water, applied with a stiff bristle brush. Rinse thoroughly with cold water and dry with a soft cloth.

Stripping Remove flaking varnish by rubbing with fine wirewool (grade 000) or use proprietary solvent-based paint stripper. Protect the framework and rinse thoroughly. When dry, buff with micro-crystalline wax for protection and lustre.

GILDED WOOD

Cleaning Gold does not tarnish so rarely needs cleaning. It is fragile, however, and vulnerable to changes in humidity. Remove dust with a soft brush. Beware: water will remove water gilding; white spirit and alcohol damage oil gilding.

GLASS

Cleaning Use concentrated technical soap (see page 172) and warm water; rinse in vinegar and water (2 tablespoons / 1 litre). Dry with a linen cloth; polish with chamois leather.

Repairs Minor chips can be rubbed down with fine wet-and-dry-sandpaper and scratches removed with a chamois leather dusted with jeweller's rouge. Glass doors on old furniture are often retained with putty; replace when necessary. It 'sticks' the glass and frame, cutting any rattle; several colours are available so some matching is possible.

LEATHER

Cleaning Dust with a soft brush and treat regularly with hide food. If very dirty, test for colour fastness and sponge carefully with saddle soap and warm water; sponge off and dry at once with a soft cloth. Or gently clean with a solution of concentrated technical soap (see page 172) and white spirit, which will not swell the leather or remove water-based dyes. Avoid cleaning gold tooling.

Repairs Red rot (a pinkish, powdery condition) should be treated with a 60/40 mixture of castor oil and alcohol and a further application of castor oil 24 hours later. Replacement desk and table tops can be ordered from specialists, custom cut to size, with gold tooled or plain edges. Where possible, retain the original, patinated leather. Unsightly scratches can usually be touched up with nitro stains (see page 137, step 6).

MARBLE

Cleaning With its porous surface marble is vulnerable to dust, stains and careless cleaning. Dust with a soft brush. Clean with a sponge soaked in a 50/50 solution of white spirit and distilled water, adding a dash of concentrated technical soap (see page 172). Sponge off with distilled water. Dry with clean cloth. To brighten white marble or conceal stains, make a paste of French chalk and distilled water, and rub into the surface until dry and burnished.

Repairs For modelling small missing parts or filling cracks and holes, use epoxy resin paste. Tint with artists' powder pigments before use for an invisible mend. For sizeable cracks, clamp the piece (see page 28) while the paste dries.

BRASS

Cleaning Excessive abrasion contributes to wear and can remove attractive patina. Choose a high-quality proprietary cleaner marked 'Long term' to reduce maintenance. Use card templates to mask surrounding wood. Old polish and dirt can be removed from crevices with cotton buds dipped in white spirit.

ORMOLU (lit. ground gold)

Cleaning Gilt bronze mounts and fittings are often used on fine French furniture and to a lesser extent on English and American pieces. Never use metal polish – this will remove the thin layer of gold. Dust with a soft brush. For ingrained dirt, use cotton buds moistened with white spirit. It is important to remember that damp conditions can cause corrosion.

Ormolu work at its best on this superb French Empire keyhole cover (c. 1805): the hand-chiselled details add a delightful 'lift' to Cuban mahogany.

MIRRORS

Cleaning Wipe with a dry linen cloth: if very dirty, use a sponge dampened with methylated spirits. Protect the frame with a cardboard template and on no account let moisture seep behind the glass. Finish with a chamois leather.

Repairs The silvery-grey reflection of old mirrored glass is highly desirable and impossible to reproduce: never be tempted to resilver antique mirrors, however scratched and pitted. Better to forget their initial function and enjoy instead the decoratively misty effect. To replace a missing or broken mirror in an old frame, investigate the 'antique' mirror ranges, which have recently improved.

Assessing just how far to go in structural repairs is a tricky stage in the restoration process. Strengthening wobbly joints is a straightforward task, usually accomplished by injecting glue and clamping or by searching out and tightening up existing screws, but more complicated consolidation should be approached with caution.

Try to put yourself in the maker's shoes. Why did he choose a particular wood or design? Did he use hand or machine tools? How did he join the piece? Make sure you have good reference books to guide you (see page 172). The answers will not only help you date the piece: they will also provide pointers as to how you should repair it.

Remember the golden rules: remove as little as possible, replace as little as possible. There are often a variety of ways in which a piece may be repaired and by choosing the least radical you are more likely to retain the initial integrity (and value) of the piece. Last but not least, bear in mind that short cuts can be the fast track to further damage.

DISMANTLING FURNITURE

Dismantling a piece of furniture can cause more damage than you had before you began: it is not, therefore, a procedure we recommend unless it is the only means to carry out a sound repair. Before starting, make sure you have a clear idea of how the piece is constructed and the best way to take it apart. Our line drawings of the commonest joints found in antique pieces may help but it is wise to research more thoroughly before taking anything apart. Have an old blanket handy to protect fragile surfaces and a marker (we use a Chinagraph which can be removed with white spirit) to label different components and simplify re-assembly.

UNRESTORED FURNITURE

Unrestored pieces, traditionally joined with pearl glue (see page 45), should be relatively easy to take apart. Quite often the glue will have perished and a few taps with a mallet will loosen the joints enough to separate them. Make sure the mallet has a rubber head – it may slow your task but it does limit further damage. Certain woods, such as rosewood and mahogany, become very brittle with age so proceed with caution to avoid splits.

If the glue remains intact, you can re-liquify it by applying moisture and heat. Use a cloth immersed in hot water and wrung out to dampen the area; then create steam with a heat gun or hairdryer. If there is still resistance, drill a small hole into the line of the joint and inject hot water using a syringe (see page 29). Bear in mind, however, that this could harm your finish and possibly lift surrounding veneer.

Pinned tenon joints A common feature on early furniture and much copied in repro pieces, a pinned tenon is a mortise and tenon joint locked together by a pin driven into a hole drilled through the mortise (or 'female' part) and the tenon (or

CONSOLIDATION

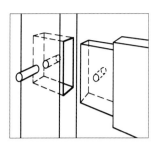

Pinned mortise and tenon joint

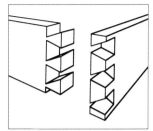

Dovetail joint

'male' part). Removing the pin is usually a case of tapping it back through. Mark each pin and its hole with Chinagraph.

Dovetail joints Use a craft knife to define the outlines. Hold a block of wood under the joint, tap with a mallet to spread the impact across the whole joint, and gently prize apart. If this does not work, place a cloth, wrung out in hot water, over the joint, renewing every 15 minutes for about an hour.

Knuckle joints See page 56. Treat as pinned tenon.

Dowel joints These are most commonly found on more recent furniture – often secured with irreversible modern glues. If this is the case, you will probably have to cut them with a gent's saw and then drill out the debris.

Half joints Since half joints are glued together rather than locked together, they can normally be separated simply by tapping or by the injection of warm water.

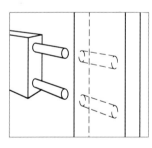

Dowel joint

Half joint

RESTORED
FURNITURE

Your principal difficulties when dismantling are likely to be caused by previous 'restoration'. The indiscriminate use of irreversible modern glues and clumsy nailing will help you understand why reversible repairs and the use of pearl glue are essential restoration practice.

Dissolving PVA glue Inject methylated spirits into the joints, using a syringe and large needle (see page 29) – again, you may have to drill a series of small holes.

Other modern glues Try injecting acetone, using the same method. Sadly, sawing is sometimes the only solution.

Removing nails and screws Always have two sets of screwdrivers by you (one set slightly sharpened) and, if possible, hollow ground – they are less likely to slip. Old brass and steel screws are often hand cut and you must make sure your screwdriver is the right size. A 25mm chisel with a V-shape filed into the tip is useful for removing nails. With the bevelled edge face down, towards the wood, place the V under the head and lever the chisel upwards to release the nail. An upholsterer's tack lifter and a sharp pair of pincers are also helpful. For really stubborn screws and nails, apply a heated soldering iron to the head, taking care not to scorch the wood. The metal will expand, force the surrounding wood fibres apart, and, when cool, contract – then simply turn the head alternately right and left to ease it out.

Applying heat alone sometimes weakens a glue joint but damping with water first speeds the process. Keep the heat gun or hairdryer moving to avoid damage to the finish.

Reversed speed clamps can apply even pressure to loosen obstinate, brittle joints. Here they are used to prise away a broken top rail. Note the protective rubber on the jaws.

MAKING AND USING HOT PEARL GLUE

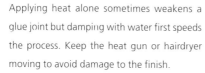

Despite the enormous range of multi-purpose glues available today, when it comes to furniture restoration nothing as yet surpasses traditional cabinet makers' glue. Known also as animal, hide, scotch, pearl or hot glue, it is now usually sold in the form of tiny brown 'pearls' – hence one of its names. We call it 'hot pearl glue'.

Minor inconveniences in its preparation and use are outweighed by its considerable advantages. First, it is easily dissolved and removed with hot water, facilitating any future repairs. If not too old, it can be re-liquified by applying heat – useful when amending repair errors. Second, it can amalgamate with itself. If cleaning off old glue proves difficult, new glue will mix and bond with the old. Third, it is flexible. Wood shifts with humidity changes and this glue will move with the wood. Fourth, it is as strong across the grain as most woods and can rival most modern glues. Fifth, it has stood the test of time. How satisfying to use the same adhesive as a craftsman of the 16th century, knowing that his work is still intact!

CONSOLIDATION

The recipe given below will make 250ml hot pearl glue. It is rarely practical to make less than this because there is always some wastage in the processes of heating and keeping warm. The small glue brush recommended (see page 31) is ideal for most jobs, but when laying sheets of veneer a larger size is convenient. Professional restorers use expensive self-heating glue pots but the improvised system we recommend here will be familiar to most cooks and is perfectly adequate. A compromise solution might be to commandeer a discarded slow cooker of the sort we regularly recruit in the service of gesso making (see page 101). You can store glue for 1 week in a fridge or 3 months in a freezer. Keep it in a clearly labelled, covered plastic container.

MATERIALS

Quantity for 250ml hot pearl glue
160g pearl glue / 140ml water to cover

EQUIPMENT

Heatproof glass bowl (see below) and saucepan / sugar thermometer / heat gun or hairdryer / small glue brush / clamps / lint-free rags

METHOD

1 Place the pearls in the glass bowl – choose a size that will fit into the top of the saucepan later – and cover with cold, clean water. Leave overnight to form a jelly.

2 Make sure the surfaces you want to join are clean well ahead of time – the glue must be used while still hot so it is important that all is ready for immediate application. Remove any traces of old glue and dirt with hot water. Avoid soaking the wood and dry at once with clean, lint-free rags.

Re-glued to repair and strengthen, this chair is speed clamped on the arm and sash clamped around the seat. To avoid marking the finish, rubber jaws have been fitted on the speed clamps and wood offcuts slipped under the sash clamps. Longer wood offcuts can also be used to spread and maintain pressure on a piece, as, for example, when gluing drawer sides (see page 66) or a jointed panel.

3 Gently heat the glue 'jelly' in the heatproof bowl over a saucepan of hot water until it has the consistency of double cream, stirring in more warm water (a little at a time) if necessary. When laying sheets of veneer, aim for a slightly thinner mix. Do not boil – 60°C (140°F) is ideal.

4 If possible and especially if your workshop is cold, warm the surfaces to be glued using a heat gun – a hairdryer will make an excellent substitute.

5 Brush the glue onto both surfaces and clamp at once if appropriate – it isn't if you are laying larger sheets of veneer (see page 89). You have to work quickly because the glue will start to cool and 'gel' within minutes. If clamping is impractical, you could use the 'rubbed-joint' method (see page 62, step 4) or heavy weights arranged on an 18mm plywood board placed over greaseproof paper.

6 Wipe away any excess glue with a damp, lint-free rag and leave to dry completely (12 hours).

STRENGTHENING JOINTS WITH GLUE

Use a syringe and large needle (see page 29) to inject hot pearl glue between as many of the joint lines as possible. Dilute the glue to make it flow more easily: it should resemble thin single cream. It helps to keep a jug of hot water beside you to warm the syringe between applications. Clamp as appropriate (see below and opposite) and leave to dry (12 hours).

USING CLAMPS

Clamps are essential for exerting a steady, even pressure upon joints, squeezing surplus glue out after gluing and for keeping the glue line thin and even. Always have a wide selection of clamps to hand (see page 28) because you can be confronted with a multitude of joints which require glue simultaneously. It is helpful to 'dry run' the clamping process before applying glue.

The uneven application of glue has unfortunate results – a wobbly chair, for example, is often a consequence of careless gluing. Another common beginner's mistake is to apply too much pressure with the clamp. This 'starves' the joint of glue, particularly when one of the glued surfaces is end grain, and can also subject the wood to harmful stress.

CHAIRS

Well over half the space in our workshop is taken up by an eclectic assortment of chairs in varying states of disrepair. It is clear why, given the bearing role they have to endure, chairs account for more repair work than any other furniture. Take time to study their construction, whether stool, plain frame or upholstered frame, and bear in mind that most chairs are designed as a series of interlocking components, linked by either mortise and tenon or dowel and socket methods of joinery (see page 43) – if one component breaks, the others are likely to follow.

REPLACING A BROKEN STRETCHER

MATERIALS **Beech blank / hot pearl glue (see page 45)**

EQUIPMENT **Electric drill with optional lip and spur bit / gouge / lathe attachment or rasp and spokeshave / dowel / 120-grade sandpaper / heatproof bowl and saucepan for warming glue / small glue brush / 2 speed clamps / wood blocks with semi-circular cut-outs to fit under-frame side rails**

METHOD

1 Drill out the broken stubs, using a slightly smaller drill diameter than that of the broken stub and setting the drill at slow speed. A lip and spur bit, if you have one, will improve accuracy.

2 Clear out any remaining splinters and old glue with a gouge.

3 Remake the missing stretcher using a beech blank, and shape with a lathe (see page 16) or by hand with rasp and spokeshave. Before cutting the blank,

Fig. 1: inserting the stretcher

make sure the new stretcher will be the right length by inserting a dowel into each of the stretcher holes to measure their depth and adding these figures to the width between the rails. Once happy with length and shape, sand smooth.

4 When ready, apply glue to each stretcher end (see page 46). Reverse the speed clamps (see page 45) to part the side under-frame rails very gently. Insert one end of the stretcher into its hole and swing the other end into place (see Fig. 1).

5 Protecting the rungs with specially cut wood blocks (see above), clamp using speed clamps (see Fig. 2). The blocks also help stabilize the clamps. Leave to dry (12 hours).

Fig. 2: clamping

EVENING UP CHAIR LEGS

Chairs that wobble are a minor but annoying problem. Before any rectification, check that uneven legs are not caused by gluing out of line. To determine which leg is the culprit, you must work on a level surface – verify it with a spirit level. A raised surface, such as a table, is ideal.

MATERIALS

If building up: block-shaped same-wood offcut(s) / hot pearl glue (see page 45)

EQUIPMENT

5 hardwood wedges cut at 2–3° angle / spirit level / pencil / re-usable adhesive mastic / gent's saw
If building up: block plane / heatproof bowl and saucepan / small glue brush / sash clamp / paring chisel

METHOD

1 Put a wedge under each chair leg and place the spirit level across the seat (Fig. 1): remember that, although on many chairs the seat is level with the floor, some seats, particularly rustic ones, slope backwards. Adjust the wedges until the chair is level.

Fig. 1: levelling

2 Check the wedges to find the shortest leg. Position the pencil on the fifth wedge and adjust until it is exactly level with the base of that leg. Secure the pencil at this point with adhesive mastic and use it to mark the other legs at the same height (Fig. 2).

3 If you find the other legs are longer by less than 3mm *and* the feet are uncarved, level them using a gent's saw. Finish as necessary.

4 If the difference is greater than 3mm or if the feet are carved, you will have to build up the short leg(s): it is possible that more than one leg is short. Clean and plane the bottom of each leg you wish to lengthen but remove only enough to provide a good gluing surface.

Fig. 2: marking the longer legs

5 Glue on a same wood offcut (see page 46), making sure the grain runs in the same direction as the leg.

6 Sash clamp (see page 47) and leave to dry (12 hours).

7 Level the offcut, using the method described above.

8 Trim with a gent's saw and paring chisel. Finish as necessary to match the existing surface.

Note Although not strictly orthodox, the bottom of chair feet can be preserved from damage and wear by self-nailing metal buttons, tapped on with a hammer.

CONSOLIDATION

GLUING A BROKEN END OF LEG

This is a relatively simple repair provided that you have the broken piece and that the break is clean, i.e. the end has snapped off in the direction of the grain without creating any 'fuzzy' edges (Fig. 1).

MATERIALS   **Hot pearl glue (see page 45)**

EQUIPMENT   **Heat gun or hairdryer / heatproof bowl and saucepan for warming glue / small glue brush / lint-free cotton rag / speed clamp with rubber jaws**

METHOD   **1** Make sure the surfaces to be glued are clean (see page 38). Check for a tight fit: if a fingernail cannot be inserted between the two pieces, then the fit is right.
2 Warm both surfaces with a heat gun or hairdryer, brush glue on both sides (see page 46) and stick together with a rubbing movement so that the fibres lock and the glue spreads evenly.

Fig. 1: clean break   Fig. 2: clamping using rubber-jaw protection

3 Immediately wipe off excess glue with a damp rag, speed clamp (see page 46) and leave to dry (24 hours). The slip-on rubber jaws are an excellent way to protect the surface.
4 If the finish has been damaged around the mend, reinstate as necessary to match the other legs.

REPLACING A BROKEN END OF LEG

When part of a chair leg is missing or too badly fractured to make a solid join, a new piece will have to be made and attached using a splice joint. This is a common, useful repair and makes an unobtrusive mend if care is taken to fit the pieces accurately and grain direction is matched. Tables can also be repaired in this way.

MATERIALS   **Same-wood offcut (see step 3) / hot pearl glue (see page 45)**

EQUIPMENT   **Block plane / tenon saw / sliding bevel / try square / pencil / paring chisel / heatproof bowl and saucepan / small glue brush / speed clamp / spokeshave**

METHOD

1 Use a block plane to remove splinters and jagged edges from the broken leg, working in the direction of the grain and taking off a minimum of wood.

2 Cut a small, angled 'hook' on the end of the broken leg, using a tenon saw.

3 With a bevel and try square, mark a reverse image of this stepped surface onto a same-wood offcut, making sure that the grain direction is matched. The offcut should be generously sized to allow for matching.

4 Cut the marked shape with a tenon saw.

5 Make a 'dry run' for fit (Fig. 1). Even up using a paring chisel until absolutely certain there is no movement.

6 Glue, clamp and leave to dry (24 hours), following the method used for Gluing a Broken End of Leg (see opposite).

7 Trim the new section with a spokeshave, chisel and block plane (Fig. 2). Check against the matching leg for accuracy.

8 Stain to match (see page 112) and finish as necessary.

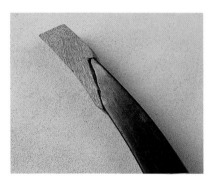
Fig. 1: checking the new section for fit

Fig. 2: trimmed and planed new section

MENDING A BROKEN MORTISE JOINT

The careless habit most of us have of tipping back in chairs puts a great deal of stress on the area where the seat rail joins the back leg, weakening the joint and eventually breaking it. To repair, the chair must be partially dismantled (see page 43) and upholstery either removed or taped back as necessary (see page 128).

MATERIALS

Same-wood offcut / hot pearl glue (see page 45)
If making blocks: beech blanks / countersink wood screws

EQUIPMENT

Paring chisel / mallet / block plane / heatproof bowl and saucepan for warming glue / small glue brush / mortise chisel
If making blocks: jigsaw / electric drill / screwdriver

METHOD

1 Clear away any splintered and fractured wood around the break (see Fig. 1, page 52), using a paring chisel, to make the smoothest possible surface for gluing.

2 Using a mallet and chisel, cut a sloped splice from a same-wood offcut – it must be a little larger than the cleared-out recess into which it should fit.

3 Position the splice in the recess and plane the shape and angles more precisely, still leaving the splice slightly proud of the existing surface. When satisfied, glue into place (see page 46), and leave to dry (12 hours).

4 Trim and shape with the paring chisel and block plane.

5 Cut out the mortises with a mortise chisel (Fig. 2).

6 Stain (see page 112) and finish to match.

7 Re-assemble the chair.

Note If your chair was made after 1850, it will probably have triangular blocks on the underside of the seat to keep the chair square and provide additional support. They are particularly necessary after this sort of repair and new blocks can be cut with a jigsaw from beech blanks and glued into place. When dry, drill and screw on for extra strength.

Fig.1 : fracture cleared of old glue

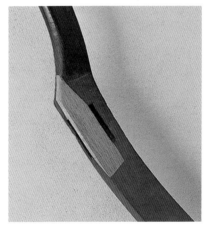

Fig. 2: new mortises on the shaped splice

MENDING A BROKEN LEG USING A JUBILEE CLIP

Turned front legs on frame chairs have a fundamental weakness: a tendency to break off at the thinner parts of the turning when subjected to excessive stress. A fault in the grain, known as 'shakes', can also be a factor. The fracture rarely takes the form of a horizontal clean break – unless the leg is affected by woodworm – but instead will splinter in a jagged vertical, and split the mortise block, which is already a weak point.

Here we show a typical break in an 1850s balloon-back chair with a stuff-over seat. As the break is recent, the splintered fibres are still intact (Fig. 1, opposite) and there are no loose or missing bits which would prevent the pieces from being closely re-fitted. It is always wise to make repairs as soon as possible after a break so that the break is less likely to be damaged further or the loose bits misplaced.

Called jubilee or hose clips, the adjustable metal clips tightened with a worm screw used here are great for securing rounded broken sections, as on turned wood, bamboo or steamed beech furniture. They are measured by diameter and sold in 12.5mm increments. The alternative: G-clamps and specially cut blocks.

Fig. 1: splintered break

Fig. 2: checking the jubilee clip for size

MATERIALS

Hot pearl glue (see page 45) / upholstery materials (see page 72)

EQUIPMENT

Strong tape / locking tape measure / jubilee clip / heatproof bowl and saucepan for warming glue / small glue brush / thick paper / scissors / screwdriver / 2 speed clamps

METHOD

1 To check for other fractures, and also to allow clamping, it will be necessary to remove the gimping (or trim) and carefully peel back the upholstery – as little as possible. Always try to preserve

Fig. 3: clamping with the clip in place

original upholstery and tape it out of the way when gluing.

2 Slot the leg back into the cleft and estimate the diameter of the join to determine the size of the jubilee clip. Make a 'dry run' with the clip to check for size (Fig. 2).

3 Remove clip and leg and apply hot pearl glue to all surfaces of the break (see page 46), including the hollowed cleft.

4 Refit the leg, shuffling it gently around in the cleft to disperse the glue evenly and lock the fibres.

5 Protect the wood with a 'collar' made from thick paper before screwing on the clip tightly. Once the clip is firmly in place, speed clamp the whole mortise block (Fig. 3 and page 47), and leave to dry (12 hours).

6 Reinstate the upholstery (see page 72).

NEOCLASSICAL CHAIR

Our furniture finds are usually rather more fanciful than this 'classic Louis Seize' *fauteuil* in painted beech, with its medallion back and seat smartly upholstered in brilliant green silk. A loose arm, revealing dowel jointing, traces of modern glue and machine marks (see page 10), meant that the chair was really showing its age – 20th-century industrial manufacturing, not 18th-century craftsmanship. This was a case, however, of 'repro' at its best, with superb quality, good proportions – the original 18th-century model was a great design – and traditional upholstery.

To begin our restoration, the PVA glue was cleaned off with methylated spirits (see page 44). The loose arm was then glued with hot pearl glue (see page 45) – even on repro – and clamped (see page 47) with G-clamps and protective blocks.

The moral of this story is that even finicky purists can have the odd lapse if the price – and the quality – is right.

TABLES

Tables have come a long way since their early form of a slab of wood supported by trestles. After the introduction of fixed legs on each corner of the slab, joined with stretchers, a great variety of styles evolved, from the relatively complex gate-leg to the elegant simplicity of the pedestal. Broken joints or legs can usually be repaired following the method used for chairs. Failed mechanical joints and cracked, warped tops require more specific repair methods.

MENDING MAJOR CRACKS IN SURFACES

Table and chest tops made from solid wood have an unfortunate tendency to split and crack, usually due to aggressive central heating or imperfect seasoning. The cracks will run along the grain and are often accompanied by warping. Although it is tempting to try to close the gaps with glue and a sash clamp, this rarely works: the crack will open up again when the clamp is removed. The traditional solution is the insertion of a butterfly key into the underside of the cracked surface to make an invisible mend. This should stabilize the crack and correct the warping.

MATERIALS

Hardwood offcut (3–6mm thick) / hot pearl glue (see page 45)

EQUIPMENT

Fretsaw / old blanket / sharp pencil / paring chisel / heatproof bowl and saucepan for warming glue / small glue brush / wooden mallet / 2 wood battens / deep-throat G-clamps

METHOD

1 Using a fretsaw, cut a wood offcut (preferably mahogany) into a butterfly shape. Make sure the grain runs from wing to wing – the opposite direction to the grain of the top (Fig. 1).

2 Reverse the table on an old blanket. Lay the butterfly shape so that it straddles the underside of the crack and draw around it with a sharp pencil to give the exact shape and position of the recess. If the crack is long, several butterfly keys may be needed: remember to number each one and its corresponding recess.

3 Cut out each recess, using a sharp paring chisel, and clear away the wood to the required depth. Test for fit but do not drop the butterfly key in – it may be difficult to retrieve.

4 Apply a thin layer of glue to the recess (see page 46) and tap in the key with a wooden mallet.

5 Finally, 'sandwich' the crack between battens, clamp with G-clamps (see page 47) and leave to dry (12 hours).

Fig. 1: note the direction of the grain

CONSOLIDATION

REPLACING THE CHASSIS ON A GATE-LEG TABLE

Gate-leg tables have proved enduringly useful throughout the last 300 years. The principle of a central chassis, from which legs pivot to support fold-up flaps, is a great example of the joiner's ingenuity, engendering any number of variations. Although the top, fold-up leaves and legs of these tables are generally made from good-quality hardwood, the hidden frame construction and pivot arrangement tend to be made from cheaper woods. This has proved to be the undoing of many gate-leg tables: not only are these woods susceptible to woodworm, but the series of open joints provide an ideal laying ground for the eggs. The damage can render the table useless and repairs will invariably entail making a new knuckle joint.

MATERIAL

Insecticide / seasoned beech / 8mm doweling / hot pearl glue (see page 45)

EQUIPMENT

Rubber hammer / heat gun or hairdryer / industrial gloves / mask / camera cleaner / 15mm household paint brush / syringe and needle (see page 29) / locking tape measure / smoothing plane / try square / steel rule / tenon saw / fretsaw / paring chisel / block plane / electric drill with 8mm auger bit / heatproof bowl and pan / small glue brush / G- and sash clamps

Fig. 1: worm-eaten chassis

METHOD

1 Dismantle the table with rubber hammer and heat gun (see page 43). Treat all pieces against woodworm (see page 36).

2 Separate the worm-eaten chassis and use the pieces to draw a series of paper templates.

3 The replacement wood – preferably well-seasoned beech of adequate length and 2mm larger all round than the original – should also be treated against woodworm.

4 Plane the lengths with a smoothing plane to remove machine marks and trim to size.

5 Mark out the 'fingers' of the new knuckle joint on the chosen length, using a try square, steel rule and pencil. Shade in the areas to be removed to avoid mistakes.

6 Very precisely, cut the horizontal sides of the shaded areas, using a tenon saw. Cut off the vertical ends with a fretsaw.

7 Assemble and check the interlocking pieces: initial stiffness will ease up so it is essential that the fit is tight. Use a paring chisel for adjustments.

8 Separate the 'fingers' and round the extremities with a block plane.

9 With an electric drill and 8mm auger bit, drill slowly through each knuckle.

10 Reassemble the pieces, insert a length of 8mm doweling through the drilled holes of the hinged pivot (Fig. 2), and cut to size.

Fig. 2: inserting doweling through pivot holes

11 Cut the new central support, modelled on the original, and glue (see page 46) to the new end blocks. Clamp with G- and sash clamps (see page 47), and leave to dry (12 hours).

12 Glue the still intact, small turned stumps at the top of the mahogany legs into corresponding holes drilled into the underside of the end blocks. Clamp as for step 11.

13 Using a tenon saw, cut tenons (see page 43) onto the end of the dismantled swinging sections of the knuckle joints. Glue into the mortises in the pivoting legs, sash clamp and leave to dry (12 hours).

14 Glue the stationary sections of the knuckle joints to the central support and G-clamp, leaving to dry (12 hours).

15 Glue the central section of the mahogany top to the central support, speed clamp and leave to dry (12 hours).

16 Replace the doweling to complete the chassis (Fig. 3).

Fig. 3: re-assembled chassis

CONSOLIDATION

CARVING A NEW LEG FOR A TRIPOD TABLE

Tripod tables frequently fail in the legs: too much weight is put on the table top, which forces the legs apart and splits the joint holding them at the base of the turned pillar. Because the legs are secured to the pillar with dovetail joints (see page 44), splits can be quite drastic: entire sections of the pillar can break off. Luckily breaks are often 'clean' and can be simply glued together again. Failing this, new timber has to be spliced into the supporting pillar. The table shown here had been damaged in this way; it was found dismantled and, although a quick check indicated that it could be satisfactorily re-assembled, a leg was missing. This is a common restoration problem, both for chairs and tables, and it is well worth learning how to carve your own replacement.

MATERIALS

3mm thick plywood / white spirit / solvent-based paint stripper / solid-wood blank / hot pearl glue (see page 45) / wood stain (see page 112)

EQUIPMENT

Pencil / fretsaw / lint-free cotton rag / 25mm house painting brush / blunted paint knife / coarse wirewool (grade 2) / smoothing plane / plywood board / speed clamp / jigsaw with long-blade attachment / paring chisel / spokeshave / profile gauge (optional) / sliding bevel / tenon saw / heatproof bowl and pan / small glue brush / rubber hammer

METHOD

1 Trace the shape of one of the existing legs onto 3mm thick plywood. Cut this template out, using a fretsaw (Fig. 1).

2 Clean and strip the existing leg (see page 38) and take it to a wood supplier. The stripped leg will help you to match up the replacement wood as closely as possible. Choose a generously wide solid-wood blank so that the new leg can be cut in the direction of the grain. This is very important both for matching and for strength.

3 Plane the wood blank with a smoothing plane to achieve the right thickness, eliminate machine marks and give an accurate guide to grain direction (Fig. 2).

4 Place the template on the wood, angling it to allow for straight grain direction on the blank. There will be wastage

Fig. 1: template for the new leg

Fig. 2: planing the wood blank

Fig. 3: drawing round the template

Fig. 4: cutting the new leg

Fig. 5: paring the dovetail joint

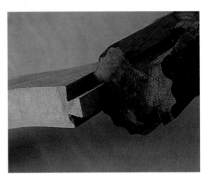

Fig. 6: checking the dovetail fits the pillar

unless you are cutting two legs which can be interfaced. Draw round the template (Fig. 3).

5 Protecting your work bench with a plywood board and speed clamping your work using the protective rubber jaws (see page 46), cut the marked-out leg using a jigsaw with a long-blade attachment (Fig. 4). You will have to adjust and re-clamp each separate portion of the leg constantly as you go round the curves.

6 Shape the cut leg cautiously, using a paring chisel and spokeshave. If necessary, check the curves using a profile gauge. Remove the clamp.

7 Use a sliding bevel and a pencil to mark out the sliding dovetail joint which attaches the leg to the central pillar. Cut it with a tenon saw and pare with a chisel (Fig. 5).

8 Slide the dovetail in to check for fit (Fig. 6). When satisfied, apply hot pearl glue (see page 46), tap the dovetail in, using a rubber hammer (Fig. 7), and leave to dry (12 hours).

9 Stain (see page 112) and finish the replacement and stripped legs to match existing finish.

Fig. 7: new leg in position

CONSOLIDATION

EXTENDING A TABLE LEG

Table legs usually need extending because they have been rashly cut down for contemporary use or have been damaged to such an extent that they are beyond repair. Since legs are the principal load bearers, the repair has to be as sturdy as possible. One solution is to fashion the end of the remaining stump into a dowel or pin which will fit into a corresponding hole drilled into the replacement part.

MATERIALS   **Same-wood section / hot pearl glue (see page 45)**

EQUIPMENT   **Chisel and rasp (for square legs) / lathe (for turned legs) / electric drill / heatproof bowl and saucepan / small glue brush / 2 sash clamps**

METHOD   **1** Research the height you wish to reinstate – this can vary slightly according to the date of the piece.
2 The same-wood replacement part must match the existing stump. Separate the top from the base (see page 43). Square legs can be repaired in the workshop: the pin should be a minimum of 3cm in length and can be formed using a chisel and rasp. For turned legs, you will have to seek help from a friendly turner if you do not have a lathe (see page 16). He or she will probably drill the corresponding hole too. Make a precise drawing of what you plan and take it with you.
3 When the dowel is carved and the hole drilled, make a 'dry run' and check for a tight fit.
4 Apply hot pearl glue to both surfaces (see page 46). Use two sash clamps to distribute the pressure evenly (see page 47) and leave to dry (12 hours).
5 Finish as necessary to match and re-assemble the table.

REGENCY TABLE

Period tables cut down to make low coffee tables are a distressing sight – the dimensions are never quite right and they can look curiously stunted – quite apart from the fact that many good tables lose their value by such changes. The Regency pedestal table shown left had been 'modernized' in this way: it amply merited restoration since its original design was superb, as was the rosewood and satinwood veneer laid in contrasting segments on a pine construction. After dismantling the table (see page 43), a new pedestal section was turned in pine, and a dowel joint constructed as described above. Hot pearl glue (see page 45) was applied to the old and new pieces, which were then joined and clamped (see page 47). An existing dark collar of veneer provided just the right decorative feature to disguise the join. The new piece was veneered, clamped using the sandbag method for curved surfaces (see page 92), and then stained (see page 112) and polished (see page 94).

CHESTS OF DRAWERS

The chest of drawers made its first appearance in the early 17th century, evolving from the easily transportable chest or *cassonne*, which until then had provided storage. Along with cabinets, sideboards and desks, it fits into the category of case furniture, a term for furniture used principally for storage and display. Drawers frequently cause problems, but it is always wise to check that the carcase is sound – take out the drawers to do the job properly – and that the feet are secure.

ADDING SUPPORT BLOCKS TO A BASE

The underside of antique case furniture is often strengthened by a series of support blocks running along the skirt. With age or damp conditions these blocks tend to fall off and should be replaced – although seemingly unimportant, they contribute quite considerably to the solidity of the whole piece. Original blocks are usually triangular, which saved on wood and maximized gluing surfaces. However, with the inevitable warping and shifting of old wood, it makes sense to use rectangular pieces – it is easier to fit them into angles which are no longer square.

MATERIALS | **Pine batten to match original dimensions / hot pearl glue (see page 45)**

EQUIPMENT | **Jack plane / locking tape measure / tenon saw / sponge / blunted paint knife / heat gun or hairdryer / heatproof bowl and pan / small glue brush**

METHOD

1 See step 1 opposite.
2 Chamfer the façade of the batten that will be exposed with a jack plane to create a 45° angle and then cut the batten into 50–75mm lengths.
3 Clean the base (see page 38), heat the surfaces you intend to stick together with a heat gun (or hairdryer) and brush with glue (see page 46).
4 Rub each block gently backwards and forwards two or three times, using a shuffling motion (Fig. 1): this action

Fig. 1: rubbing the blocks in

pushes the glue into the wood fibres and squeezes out any remaining air, increasing adhesion on the surfaces. Once in position, leave to dry (12 hours).

REPLACING A BRACKET FOOT

Bracket feet on old chests can give the illusion of being more substantial than they really are – in fact they are often just a decorative device. As with all feet on furniture they are vulnerable to damage, whether through damp conditions, woodworm and rot or clumsy displacement. Here we replace the foot on a mahogany-veneered Georgian chest, using a method that can be easily adapted to your particular piece.

CHESTS OF DRAWERS

MATERIALS

Pine board for brackets / pine batten for glue blocks / wood block for foot / hot pearl glue (see page 45)

EQUIPMENT

Blanket / locking tape measure / cardboard / fretsaw / tenon saw / jack plane / heatproof bowl and pan / small glue brush / block plane (optional)

METHOD

1 Remove all the drawers and carefully turn the empty chest upside down, laying it on an old blanket to protect the top.

2 Make a cardboard template from an existing bracket. If all of them are missing, research an appropriate shape in reference books.

3 Cut two brackets, using a fretsaw. We used 18mm pine to match the pine carcase and an existing bracket.

4 Measure one of the existing square feet and cut another to match, making it 6mm longer than the new bracket.

5 Cut the two glue blocks to size – flush with the sides of the brackets when they are assembled with the foot. 'Dry run' for fit and then chamfer (as opposite) all internal edges (Fig. 1).

Fig. 1: replacement brackets, blocks and foot

Fig. 2: applying glue to the foot

Fig. 3: rubbing in the glue blocks

6 Rub in the brackets on the underside of the chest, using the method described opposite (step 4).

7 Next rub in the foot (Fig. 2), taking care not to disturb the pieces already rubbed in. Although the glue is set, it is still in a jelly state and the bond could easily be broken.

8 Finally rub in the two glue blocks, carefully supporting the main structure while sliding the blocks backwards and forwards (Fig. 3). Leave to dry (12 hours).

9 Trim the shaped bracket pieces with a block plane if necessary, veneer to match the chest (see page 89, Hammer Veneering) and then finish.

CONSOLIDATION

REPAIRING A DRAWER BASE

The solid wood bottoms of early drawers were normally made so that the grain ran from front to back. In later drawers the bottom was set in grooves and the grain ran from side to side. Later still, as drawers got thinner and lighter, the bottom was set in a channel formed by drawer slips, with the grain running from side to side. If the wood shrinks, the ensuing cracks will run along the direction of the grain and most likely divide the glue lines joining the two or three thin boards that make up the drawer base. Glue lines are also inevitably weakened by humidity changes.

MATERIALS

Hot pearl glue (see page 45) / 2 panel pins / candle

EQUIPMENT

Heatproof bowl and saucepan / small glue brush / speed clamps / jack plane hammer

METHOD

1 Remove the drawer – it may well fall apart.
2 Re-assemble the dovetail sides, using hot pearl glue (see page 46). Speed clamp (see page 47); leave to dry (12 hours).
3 Hold the broken pieces of the base together against the light to check fit – even up with a jack plane. Clamp the lower half verticallly and rub in the upper half (Fig. 1 and page 62, step 4). Leave to dry in this position (12 hours).
4 To replace the base, clamp the front of the drawer in an upright position and carefully slide the base in (Fig. 2). Beginners often glue the base into the side grooves, forgetting that wood needs space to expand and contract.

Fig. 1: rubbing in the upper half

Fig. 2: sliding in the drawer base

5 Tap two small pins through the base into the back corners of the drawer to secure.
6 Before replacing the drawer, rub a candle along the drawer runners and the drawer sides to ease the movement.

Note To repair a small crack on a drawer base, glue an open-weave canvas strip to the underside of the crack.

REPLACING WORN RUNNERS ON A DRAWER

Since the late 17th century many drawers have been constructed to run on two strips of wood attached to the sides of the carcase. With the weight of contents, and the frequency of use, these become very worn: the drawer no longer runs smoothly or becomes mis-aligned, leading to other problems, such as torn frontal veneer. Slivers of new wood can be let in to build up the worn runners, but it is tricky work for an amateur, and could end up causing further damage. We recommend two alternatives.

MATERIALS

Hot pearl glue (see page 45) / pine fillets (optional) / flat-headed nails

EQUIPMENT

Choose as appropriate: old mortise chisel / locking tape measure / pencil / tenon saw / heatproof bowl and saucepan for warming glue / small glue brush / hammer / speed clamps / sash clamp

METHOD

1 Old runners are generally held in by glue and hand-made, square-headed pins, which are difficult to remove. Prize the runners out gently with a chisel. Do not apply heat to melt the glue – this could damage the finish on the outside.

2 Turn the runners to expose a new surface and glue them back in (see page 46). If this is not possible, cut and glue in new runners, using the existing ones as templates.

3 Pin the turned or new runners in, using flat-headed nails which, although historically inaccurate and not for the finest pieces, will ensure that the runners can be easily repaired.

Fig. 1: clamping the runners using a reversed speed clamp

4 Clamping inside carcases presents difficulties due to the restricted space. The best solution is to use the carcase itself to brace the clamps. This is done by reversing a speed clamp and bracing it against the side or central support (Fig. 1). Apply only light pressure to the glued runner – too much force could damage the carcase. To avoid any risk, put a sash clamp on the corresponding exterior. Leave to dry (12 hours).

CONSOLIDATION

REPAIRING WORN DRAWER SIDES

On lighter-weight chests of the 18th and 19th centuries, carcasing and all working parts were made in pine; oak and mahogany were reserved for the more expensive pieces. Pine, a softwood, is subject to considerable wear, which can lead to scooped edges along the bottom of the sides of drawers. This, in turn, can cause 'knock-on' damage and should be repaired. Although it is permissible to replace drawer runners (see page 65), it is not good practice to replace worn drawer sides, which are an important part of the piece's history.

MATERIALS

Pine slivers / hot pearl glue (see page 45)

EQUIPMENT

Paring chisel / block plane / locking tape measure / pencil / tenon saw / heatproof bowl and saucepan for warming glue / small glue brush / speed clamps / large batten

METHOD

1 Working on one side at a time, chisel and plane the damaged area using a paring chisel and a block plane.
2 Cut a slightly oversized pine sliver with a tenon saw and glue into place (see page 46). Matching the wood to the drawer sides is vital. Harder wood can cause runners to fail.
3 Speed clamp the repair (see page 47), using a large batten to distribute the pressure, and leave to dry (12 hours).
4 When the repair is dry, trim the sliver, using a block plane.

Note It is essential not to nail the face of any moving part of a drawer assembly because the nail head will eventually wear through and cause considerable damage to the runner.

The upper drawer shows wear to the base of the drawer side. The lower drawer shows the new sliver glued in and speed clamped. A pine batten is used to distribute the pressure.

METAL FITTINGS

Appropriate – or inappropriate – metal fittings can make or break a piece of furniture, and it's amazing how often this essential part of restoration gets overlooked or underestimated. Handles, hinges, castors and locks often serve not just a useful function, but a decorative one as well – on antique furniture these elements were carefully thought out as an integral part of the whole design. When choosing replacements, spend time researching the correct style for your piece: mail-order catalogues from specialist suppliers (see page 172) offer a surprisingly wide, and internationally viable, choice of fittings, which you can then compare with illustrated reference books. Measure carefully and make a paper template to check proportions before ordering.

This drawer, from a late 18th-century English mahogany desk, had been 'dressed up' with a reproduction early 18th-century brass handle, which we removed; it can now be seen lying in the foreground. It was not only misleading but also covered up an original keyhole. Research was needed to find an appropriate handle.

MOULDING A BACK PLATE

Missing handles and drawer pulls usually follow a standard design and can be easily replaced. Back plates, key escutcheons and decorative metal mounts can, however, prove more elusive: here we show how to make a very plausible copy, using a polyester resin mixed with metal filler. Although there is an initial outlay for materials, amounts needed are very small and you can make several fittings. Plumber's silicone, sold in a tube, could replace the polyester resin but it will take a week to dry. Here we make a replacement back plate for a late 18th-century chest of drawers, using an original plate as a model.

MATERIALS | 150ml silicone moulding rubber and catalyst to suit / 45ml polyester resin and catalyst to suit / 2tbsp brass filler / metal polish

EQUIPMENT | Spirit-resistant vinyl gloves / mask / screwdriver / plasticine / A4 paper / masking tape / 2 flexible plastic containers / hacksaw / 120-grade sandpaper / electric drill and metal bit / fine wirewool (000) / soft cloth

METAL FITTINGS

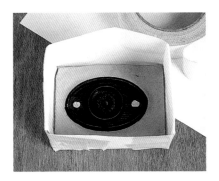

Fig. 1: plate pushed into the plasticine

Fig. 2: pouring moulding mixture into the box

Fig. 3: rubber mould

Fig. 4: pouring the resin and filler mixture

METHOD

WEAR GLOVES AND A MASK. WORK IN A WELL-VENTILATED SPACE.

1 Unscrew one of the original plates.

2 Form a flat rectangle of plasticine – slightly larger than the plate – and place it on a sheet of A4 paper. Fold the sides up to form an open box, securing with masking tape.

3 Push the plate down, face up, on the plasticine (Fig. 1), making sure any holes are flush to prevent the moulding fluid leaching under the plate.

4 Mix the rubber moulding materials to the manufacturer's instructions in one of the plastic containers and pour slowly into the box, starting in the centre (Fig. 2) and covering the whole box to a depth of 1cm. Leave to dry (4–24 hours).

5 Remove the paper box, plasticine and plate. You will find a clear imprint of the plate on the rubber mould (Fig. 3).

6 Using the other plastic container, mix up 3 tablespoons polyester resin with its catalyst, following the manufacturer's instructions. Stir in the brass filler.

7 Pour the mixture slowly onto the centre of the mould (Fig. 4), using enough to cover just the plate with a slightly raised pool. Leave to set for twice as long as stated in the manufacturer's instructions.

8 Peel the rubber mould off the new resin plate, which will be a dreary brown colour. Trim off surplus edges with a hacksaw and sand the edges and the back.

9 Use an electric drill, fitted with a suitable metal bit, to make holes for the screws.

10 Rub with wirewool until the brass filler begins to gleam.

11 Use an abrasive metal polish and soft cloth to shine, and 'antique' (see below).

Q: Can you spot the difference?
A: It is often very nearly impossible to distinguish between the metal back plate (lower drawer) and the antiqued, new resin moulding (upper drawer). The only give-away can be a slightly duller sound when you tap the resin moulding with a fingernail.

ANTIQUING NEW METAL FITTINGS

For restorers, brand-new fittings have a most unwelcome gleam, and the ready-made 'antique' alternative can be equally disconcerting. The solution is to buy standard fittings and 'age' them using a proprietary cold-patination product.

MATERIALS

Solvent-based paint stripper / white spirit / cold-patination fluid (brown) / micro-crystalline wax

EQUIPMENT

Spirit-resistant vinyl gloves / household paint brush / lint-free cotton rag / mask / cottonwool / fine wirewool (grade 000)

METHOD

WEAR GLOVES AND MASK. WORK IN A WELL-VENTILATED SPACE.

1 Strip the inevitable coat of modern lacquer by brushing on solvent-based paint stripper with a household paint brush.

2 Remove with rag and neutralize with white spirit.

3 Once dry, use cottonwool to dab on the patination fluid randomly for a natural effect. The surface instantly darkens.

4 Stop as soon as the desired effect is achieved – this could vary between 30 seconds and several minutes.

5 Rinse in water and dry with a lint-free cotton rag.

6 Buff high spots with wirewool for a well-worn look.

7 Protect with micro-crystalline wax, applied with a rag.

Fig. 1:
before (top) and after

METAL FITTINGS

REPLACING A PIVOT HINGE

Pivots are found on the top and bottom edges of wardrobe or cabinet doors, and are set into the thickness of the door for invisibility. If your hinge is not working, always check first for dirt or rust: cleaning and oiling could be all that is required. Replacing hinges is not complicated, although the correct way to remove a pivot hinge is not immediately obvious. In some countries the releasing screws are removed from above, in others from below. The principle is exactly the same

EQUIPMENT **Screwdriver**

METHOD **1** Find the position of the releasing screws on one of the hinges. You can determine this by touch.
2 In order to free the screwed section, remove the one or two screws visible when the door is fully open and hold the door at a right angle to the carcase.

Fig.1: replacement hinge and slot   Fig.2: sliding the door into position

3 Slide out the screwed section and the other section will follow. (It has no retaining screws and simply slides out too.)
4 To replace the hinge, reverse this procedure (Figs. 1 and 2).

MAKING A NEW KEY FOR A WARD LOCK

Most 18th- and 19th-century furniture was fitted with locks; often a piece had only one key, although desks could have several. Keys do go missing, but can be replaced more easily if the lock is a ward lock. The ward lock was commonly used on 18th-century furniture, and modest 19th- and even 20th-century pieces. A hollow pipe runs along the top of the key blade: when the blade is inserted in the lock, the pipe fits over a central pin. When the key is turned, a notch on the blade will ride over a protruding flange on the lock plate, causing the bolt to shoot out.

MATERIALS **2 key blanks**

EQUIPMENT **Screwdriver / cardboard to 'file' screws / metal file / re-usable adhesive mastic / vice / hacksaw**

METAL FITTINGS

METHOD

1 Unscrew the lock carefully, 'filing' the screws for replacement at the end.

2 Take the lock to a hardware store or locksmith and choose a key blank which fits over the central pin. It should not be too tight, but the blade can be longer than the slot designed for it. It is always wise to buy two blanks to allow for mistakes when cutting to fit.

3 Trim the blade of the key blank with a metal file, so that it fits into the slot lengthwise – it will not fit depth-wise at this stage because of the protruding flange.

4 To calculate the position of the notch on the blade, stick a piece of adhesive mastic on to the blade and drop it back into the lock (Fig. 1): the flange will make a clear impression on the adhesive.

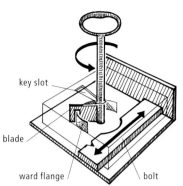

Ward-lock mechanism
(simplified)

Fig. 1: locating the notch

Fig. 2: cutting the key

5 Place the key handle in a vice and, using a hacksaw, cut out the shallow impression made on the mastic (Fig. 2).

6 To ensure the notch is deep enough, drop the blade, with mastic re-attached, back into the lock. If the flange marks the mastic, use a hacksaw to cut the notch a little deeper and then test again, repeating until no further marks appear.

7 Turn the key in the lock a number of times to test that the mechanism is working.

Note Inappropriate key handles can easily be replaced, and for little cost, with decorative brass handles in a style that complements your piece. Cut the original handle off with a hacksaw and fit the new handle in place. Fix with a pin, or glue into place with epoxy resin. A silk tassel gives an added flourish and guards against further loss.

UPHOLSTERY

Until quite recently, upholstery was something of a 'poor relation' among the multiple crafts that make up furniture restoration. It was common practice to lovingly restore an antique chair frame, whilst tearing off its original upholstery and replacing it with a poorly-researched fabric on a foam-rubber base. There is now an increasing awareness that re-upholstering old pieces – including marvellously over-stuffed Victoriana – needs a sensitive and informed approach, using techniques appropriate to the period and style of the piece. There are many specialized books on upholstery, both practical and historical, and an ever-widening choice of re-edited period fabrics, in designs and colourways as fresh and daring as anything dreamt up today.

If you are a beginner, we recommend restricting yourself to relatively simple work, such as the techniques shown here. A minimum of tools should include a staple gun – although in no way traditional, it is fast, efficient and, most importantly, causes considerably less damage to fragile frames than tacks do. Nylon thread also departs from tradition but is strong, will never rot, and pulls through more easily. Wear a hand protector when tightening edge stitching: an old leather glove with the fingers cut off is ideal.

REPLACING A STUFF-OVER SEAT

The stuff-over seat, with its generous layers of stuffing and firmly defined edges, successfully combines both comfort and durability, and is particularly suitable for heavy-duty seating, such as dining chairs. It is based on traditional 18th-century methods and forms the foundation for other forms of upholstery. Here we use it to upholster an early Victorian chair.

MATERIALS	3m x 5cm webbing / 1m x 130cm heavyweight hessian / upholsterer's nylon thread / 350g sifted coconut fibre / 1m x 130cm medium-weight hessian / 350g curled hair / 1m x 140cm linter felt wadding / 1m x 140cm calico / 1m x 140cm cloth for top cover / 2m x 15mm gimping / fabric glue or gimping pins
EQUIPMENT	Tack lifter / mallet / hand-held staple gun / webbing stretcher / scissors / tape measure / curved upholsterer's needle / regulator / 25cm double-pointed straight needle / hand protector / upholstery hammer (optional)
METHOD Removing the upholstery	Removing old upholstery is a vital part of the restoration process (see page 126). Throw nothing away immediately – you may need to make a template or check for reference.
Webbing	This provides the essential upholstery support, so it is important to position and fix it correctly. Depending on the shape of the frame, you may have to fan the webbing out. Research international differences too – on French furniture, for instance, there is no space left between the webbing.

1 Place the chair on the work bench. Working directly from the roll of webbing, make a 3cm turn at the loose end and staple it, face up, at the centre of the back rail.

2 Using the webbing stretcher, pull the webbing taut to the centre of the front rail, staple, turn, cut and fix as before.

3 Continue, fixing webbing on either side of the first piece.

4 Fix the side webbing in the same way, weaving it alternately over and under at the 'crosses' (Fig. 1).

Fig. 1: stretching the webbing

Hessian base

1 Cut a square of heavyweight hessian to match the chair frame, adding a 5cm allowance all round.

2 Place over the webbing and staple tautly, stretching from back to front and then from side to side. You must create an even tension for this additional support. Trim, leaving a 3cm allowance all round, turn over and staple again.

3 Using a curved needle, tie a slip knot at one of the back corners of the webbing and make a series of back-stitched loops through the base and the webbing, working across the chair (Fig. 2). These loops, called bridle ties, fix the stuffing and prevent it from moving.

Coconut fibre

1 Take a handful of coconut fibre and push it under the loops, working from the back towards the front (Fig. 3). Continue until the whole frame is covered.

2 Use a regulator to tease and distribute the fibre evenly, making sure that there is plenty around the edges. Flatten your palm against the fibre to check for sparse areas.

Fig. 2: making the bridle ties

Fig. 3: coconut fibre through the bridle ties

This 18th-century French (Louis Seize) chair has been upholstered in a modern variation of a period fabric. Although care has been taken to match the grey and rose fabric with soft grey paintwork, stripes, as can be seen, are a difficult choice when used for stuff-over chairs.

Medium-weight hessian covering

1 Cut a square of hessian to cover all the coconut fibre, adding a 5cm allowance all round.

2 Working from the centre, tuck in and staple a 3cm turning along the back rail. Making sure the weave remains square to the frame, pull the fabric tautly forwards and secure with widely spaced temporary staples above the front show wood. Continue, working the sides in the same way.

3 Once secure and square, trim the front and sides, leaving 3cm all round. Replace the temporary staples, one at a time, tucking the fabric in and restapling.

4 Cut the hessian diagonally across the back corners and snip out a small 'V' shape centred on the middle of the leg (Fig. 4). Keeping the fabric smooth, tuck it under neatly.

5 Cut the front corners in the same way. Turn the hessian under, working from front to side, smooth and staple.

6 Work the regulator through the hessian to ensure the fibre still has an even density, particularly at the edges, where it should slightly overhang.

7 Make a series of loose top stitches in the opposite direction to the bridle ties, running a straight needle through the hessians and webbing. Then pull them tight to compress the stuffing and stabilize the whole central area. Regulate the edges of the pad again.

Edge stitching

1 With the regulator, make a series of holes, 2cm apart, along the top edge and sides of the pad: these will guide the edge stitching.

Fig. 4: cutting the corners [note top stitching in position]

2 Thread a double-pointed needle with nylon thread. Insert it up through the second set of holes from the left back leg, push it down through the first set of holes, and secure with a slip knot (Fig. 5).

3 Push the needle up through the third set of holes (Fig. 6), pulling it right through and leaving approximately 10cm of slack at the bottom. Push the needle backwards – eye first – partway down through the second set of holes. Loop the left side of the slack under and over the lower part of the needle, repeat with the right side of the slack (Fig. 7), and then pull the rest of the needle through. Tighten the thread to lock the stitch. The seat changes shape as the edges are sharpened.

4 Continue around the edges of the chair, following the same method. Tie off when each edge is complete.

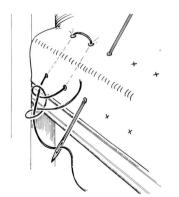

Fig. 5: securing with a slip knot

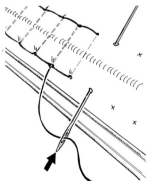

Fig. 6: 'up' stitch

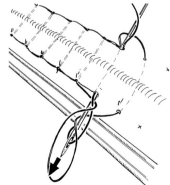

Fig. 7: looping the thread

Fig. 8: inserting the curled hair

Fig. 9: smoothed calico covering

Curled hair and wadding

1 Sew bridle ties as before. Place the curled hair on the seat, teasing it with the regulator and tucking it into the ties (Fig. 8).
2 Lay the linter felt wadding over the curled hair and trim it to the shape of the seat.

Calico lining

1 Cut the calico lining to cover the linter felt wadding completely, allowing a 5cm overlap all round.
2 Making sure the weave of the calico remains square, and that it is pulled taut and smooth across the seat, staple the lining on to the chair rails (Fig. 9). Trim.
3 Tuck in the back corners as for the medium-weight hessian. For the front corners, make a neat fold, cut a small inverted 'V', and tuck in before fixing.

Top cover

To avoid mistakes, wait until the pad is complete before measuring the fabric for the top cover.

1 Lay the fabric so that the weave is exactly square, and staple on to the seat rails and trim, taking care to establish the straight line of show wood.
2 Make the corners, following the methods used for the calico.
3 Stick on gimping using fabric glue, or gimping pins if you need to match an existing set of chairs (Fig. 10).

Fig. 10: gimping

REPLACING A DROP-IN SEAT

The simple stuffed pad on a removable seat frame has been in frequent use since the late 17th century, and learning how to make it is a useful repair for both antique and more contemporary chairs. Although some of the basic principles are the same as those for the stuff-over seat, the drop-in seat provides an easier starting point for beginners.

MATERIALS

2½m x 5cm webbing / ½m x 140cm heavyweight hessian / upholsterer's nylon thread / 350g sifted coconut fibre / 350g polished black fibre / ½m x 140cm shredded cotton wadding / ½m x 140cm polyester wadding / ½m x 140cm calico / 1m x 140cm cloth for top cover

EQUIPMENT

G-clamp / wood offcuts / hand-held staple gun / webbing stretcher / scissors / tape measure / curved upholsterer's needle / regulator

METHOD
Checking the frame

If your frame is still intact, check that it fits properly and is not warped or infested (see page 36). If the frame cannot be used, a new one will have to be made (see page 167).

Webbing and hessian base

Follow the stuff-over method (see page 72). When webbing, clamp the frame to your work bench with a G-clamp.

Stuffing

1 Tuck the coconut fibre under the bridle ties, thinning it at the edges.
2 Cover with a layer of polished black fibre, again working it under the bridle ties, and using the regulator to ensure a good, even distribution.
3 Cut a square of cotton wadding to cover and shape it with your fingertips so that it 'locks' into the preceding layers. Check with your flattened palm for any lumps or hollows and fill.
4 Cut a square of polyester wadding to just cover the top, making sure that it does not hang over the sides (Fig. 1). This avoids unnecessary bulk.

Fig. 1: four layers of stuffing

Undercover

1 Cut calico to cover the seat, allowing an extra 6cm all round.
2 Stretch it firmly and smoothly over the seat and staple to the underside.
3 For neat corners, cut a small inverted 'W' into each right angle and staple the central 'V' to the underside (Fig. 2).

Fig. 2: fixing a corner

Fold one of the long arms of the 'W' over and staple. Repeat with the other.

3 Once all four sides are completed, trim the excess fabric to reduce bulk.

Fig. 3: completed corners

Top cover

1 Measure the fabric for the top cover, allowing an extra 5cm all round.

2 It is very important to fix the fabric accurately and squarely on the seat – particularly when it is decorated with a large central motif. The solution is simple: mark the exact centre of all four frame rails with a pencil; mark the fabric too, using a needle and thread. Now align those marks as you place your fabric.

3 Staple the top fabric onto the underside of the back rail.

4 Pull the fabric towards the front rail, making sure the tension is firm but not too tight.

5 Staple temporarily and fix the sides in the same way.

6 Once you are happy with the fit, secure the fabric with more staples, making the corners as before, and trim.

LEATHER CHAIR

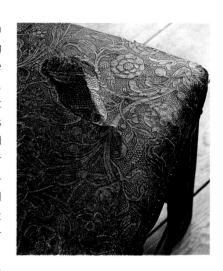

'Revival' style furniture of the 19th century can make for some amusing and inexpensive finds. A label on the underside of this chair, one of a pair, told us it was made in Germany, in that popular style endearingly known as 'Historismus'. With a straight-backed walnut frame and embossed leather upholstery, it made a stab at 17th-century authenticity, but the damaged seat revealed rather more prosaic stuffing than the grass, straw and deer hair which was used at that time!

Curiously placed plugged mortise joints on the upper part of the chair frame indicated that the decoratively carved backs had once been part of another, quite different, piece of furniture. Closer inspection revealed hand-carved details, in contrast to the other, machine-made components. Pieces such as these, incorporating bits of decorative old wood into a newer structure can be misleading for the unwary buyer, who imagines he or she is purchasing the 'real thing'. When buying furniture, always look at the piece as a whole and make sure that individual components match up.

To mend the tear, the nails holding the leather to the front rail were removed with a tack lifter, working with the grain. The leather was gently peeled – not folded – back, to limit any damage. A generously cut muslin square was brushed lightly with a weak solution of PVA glue and then stuck over the tear. After 2 hours, glue was re-applied. When dry, the seat was re-nailed and cleaned (see page 41).

PART TWO

SURFACES

Detailed, step-by-step instructions for the restoration techniques and traditional skills you need to repair or reinstate surface finishes, whether on wood – ranging from a simple recipe for reviving an unloved piece, through staining or coping with significant blemishes, to replacing sheet veneer and then French polishing or waxing the replacement part – on gilding or original paintwork

An engraved glass seems to float on the polished surface of this old mahogany table. Years of use and loving care have given the wood a warm, translucent glow – a few minor blemishes here and there merely add to its history and to a sense of the piece's ongoing life.

SURFACE REPAIRS

Once structural repairs are out of the way, you will find yourself having to make a few decisions about how far you wish to take the restoration process. It is evident that after decades – or possibly even centuries – of constant use, the surface of your piece will no longer be in a pristine condition: with luck it will have aged beautifully and acquired a mellow patina. There might be a few minor knocks and dents, the odd veneer patch or wax-filled hole, even a replacement part or two – all respectable signs of a lifetime's service. The importance of patina cannot be over-emphasized – although it can be imitated convincingly, nothing can ever replace the precious imprint of time or the highly desirable character of furniture left to age gracefully.

Take the time to step back from the piece and ask a few questions. Is the surface finish appropriate to the piece? Is it the original finish? Could it be left as it is, with perhaps a clean and polish, or are there other problems to be addressed? Can stripping be avoided? Always remember that the restorer – and not just the amateur restorer – can be over-zealous in his or her work and forget that the boundary between restoration and renewal is dangerously thin. It is for this reason that you should carefully define which surface flaws and blemishes are acceptable and which should be eradicated. Knowing what to remove and what to leave requires experience and a degree of sensitivity – it is also a question of taste.

Once those decisions are made, your first step in this process will be to remove any surface imperfections you consider intolerable. A summary of these often minor problems, and appropriate solutions, begins opposite, with particular reference to French polished surfaces, which are notoriously vulnerable to both heat and water.

MAKING AND APPLYING REVIVER

Reviver enhances the grain and, once the surface is dry, re-establishes the shine. Professional restorers tend to make up their own, and recipes vary considerably. We use a simple, effective formula called 'half and half', composed of 1 part raw linseed oil, 1 part white spirit and a dash of vinegar. The drop of vinegar cuts through any grease, the white spirit dissolves the top layer of polish, and the linseed oil lubricates the whole process. However, for small quantities we recommend you buy a proprietary brand: a wide range is readily available. Some contain pumice and even ammonia. Use them only as a last resort.

Apply with a soft, lint-free cotton cloth, using a circular motion and wiping occasionally with a clean cloth. A word of warning: linseed oil, if allowed to sink in, will darken wood and give an uneven effect if the old finish is cracked or patchy. Make sure you rub off all traces of the oil.

SOLVING COMMON PROBLEMS

Dull finish   Tired and shabby-looking pieces can be smartened up with a solution known in the trade as a reviver (see opposite).

Blooming   When left in cold, damp spaces, a milky cloud appears on French polished and varnished furniture. To remove, clear off any wax with white spirit. If the bloom remains unchanged, use a reviver (see opposite).

White water marks   This is localized blooming and can look quite dramatic. If the surface is wax finished, try rubbing new wax in with fine wirewool (grade 000). For French polished surfaces, clean with white spirit and use a reviver (see opposite). If the marks persist, use a few drops of raw linseed oil, worked along the grain with superfine wirewool (grade 0000). Be careful not to cut below the surface layer. Wipe off any traces of oil with clean rags. In certain instances, water will deteriorate the French polished surface to such an extent that stripping is the only alternative (see page 39).

Abandoned for years in a shed, the surface of this chair was apparently ruined. Covered in whitish bloom (a reaction to the polish) and lifeless, it comes as a surprise that it can be simply revived (see opposite).

Black water, spirit and ink stains   When water, spirits or ink are left to seep right through a finish and into the wood, unsightly black marks are inevitable. If the marks are very large, you might have to strip the surface and bleach (see pages 39 and 86). Bear in mind that, although the stain might not be totally removed, it should blend in quite successfully when the finish is replaced.

Cigarette burns/ scorch marks   Burns are rarely 'skin' deep – in most cases they burn through the finish and damage the wood underneath, making a blackened indentation. Iron objects, when left on oak, will leave grim 'scorch' marks. Both small and large areas can be patched (see page 87).

Crazing   This affects French polished surfaces and is usually caused by furniture being left in direct sunlight. Clean the surface with fine wirewool (grade 000) and white spirit. Carefully, using a rubber (see page 95), apply methylated spirits to the top layer of polish. This softens the polish and causes it to dissolve and re-form. When dry and hard, re-polish to blend (see page 96, Bodying up) – one layer will be enough.

Orange-peel effect This is usually caused by French polish being applied over another finish (a common mistake in the 19th century, when the French polishing technique was relatively new). Usually the only solution will be to strip (see page 39) and renew the finish (see page 94).

Worn edges An example of something we prefer to leave alone: fakers go to great lengths to achieve this effect and with good reason.

Dents Soft woods, such as pine, are prone to dents. To remove, fold pieces of damp rag over the area and heat the rag with a domestic iron, pre-set at medium. Repeat several times, dampening the rag on each occasion. Do not use this method over high-quality surface finishes.

TRIPOD TABLE

Tripod tables were made by the thousands on both sides of the Atlantic during the 18th century – they were the perfect occasional table, serving a multitude of purposes, from candle-holder stands to breakfast tables. It was tea-drinking, however, newly introduced during this period, that gave these tables their most popular and enduring function. Usually made in mahogany or oak, their tops could be flipped up or down, facilitating their passage through narrow doors and reminding us that, in the past, furniture, when not in use, was arranged against reception room walls. The tripod has the further advantage of stability on uneven floors.

This solid mahogany table had stood for years in a south-facing window, serving principally as a vase stand. The result was an unattractive, sun-bleached, water-marked surface. Our aim was to remove these very obvious marks but maintain, nevertheless, its antique appearance. As with many 18th-century pieces, the French polish finish had been applied at a later date, probably in the 19th century. We decided to retain this, since it enhanced the mahogany and meant only the damaged top would have to be stripped (see page 39) and bleached. One application (see page 86) was sufficient to remove the worst of the rings – we could have bleached further, but chose to retain the slight imperfections and, more importantly, the colour of the wood. The top was then French polished (see page 94) and, to our wry amusement, the owner placed the newly restored table firmly back in its old position.

SURFACE REPAIRS

LIGHTENING WOOD AND BLEACHING STAINS

Although natural fading on furniture can be desirable, care should be taken when artificially lightening wood: bleaching processes can leave wood looking like lifeless driftwood. For restoration purposes, these can be useful, however, for removing stains, or for lightening a replacement piece when restoring pale coloured woods.

For minor stains on wood, domestic bleach can be used, dabbed on undiluted and then washed off with cold water. For deeply penetrative stains, such as ink, or iron marks on oak, the ready-made, two-part alkaline A and B bleach packs are effective on stripped surfaces. Take care, however, as they are not always as predictable as stated. (The more traditional oxalic acid crystals should not be used as they are difficult to find and highly poisonous.) Remember that bleaches affect different woods in varying ways: it is advisable to experiment on a same-wood offcut when possible.

Fig. 1: before treatment

MATERIALS **A and B bleach pack / 1tbsp vinegar per 500ml cold-water solution**

EQUIPMENT **Spirit-resistant vinyl gloves / mask / synthetic (white nylon) brush**

Fig. 2: first application

METHOD WEAR GLOVES AND A MASK. WORK IN A VENTILATED SPACE.

1 Clean and strip the surface (see page 38).

2 To the stripped surface (Fig. 1), apply the A (activator) solution, using the synthetic brush and following the manufacturer's instructions. Leave to work for 20 minutes.

3 Apply the B (bleaching) solution liberally, using the same (washed) brush, and leave (3 hours minimum).

4 Rinse with water and check the colour (Fig. 2). If the stain is still dark, allow the wood to dry and repeat the process. It may not be possible to remove a stain completely (Fig. 3), but once the surface has been re-finished it will blend satisfactorily with the surrounding wood.

5 Brush on vinegar and water to neutralize the pH.

Fig. 3: second application

FILLING SCRATCHES AND MINOR CRACKS

For restoration purposes we tend to use wax and shellac sticks – they are problem-free, easy to use, and have the advantage of being reversible. Ideally suited to filling in cracks, pits and scratches, they are sold in a variety of colours to use alone or mix. Wax sticks have a low melting point – useful when repairing heat-sensitive finished pieces. Shellac sticks – with a high melting point – work best on unfinished pieces.

MATERIALS   Wax or shellac stick

EQUIPMENT   Low-wattage soldering iron / tongue spline / clean linen cloth

METHOD   **1** Heat the soldering iron (an inexpensive and useful tool).
2 When hot, hold the iron over the crack and press the wax against the tip of the blade. Allow the drips that form to fall into the crack where they quickly cool and harden (Fig. 1).

Fig. 1: dripping wax into the crack

Fig. 2: removing excess wax

3 Keep the soldering iron moving along the crack, making sure it does not get too hot – it will burn and blacken the wax if it does. Switch off and allow to cool from time to time before continuing.
4 Carefully scrape off excess wax with a tongue spline (Fig. 2). Any residue can be removed by friction polishing with a clean linen cloth (Fig. 3).

Fig. 3: polishing the repair

PATCHING SMALL AND LARGE BURNS

Small burns Glue a sandpaper patch onto the end of a dowel and rub gently to remove the charred area. Repair the hole with a wax stick (see above) and level with a tongue spline.
Large burns Cut out with a paring chisel, removing the groundwork under veneered surfaces if also affected. To fill groundwork, cut a same-wood plug, glue (see page 45) and level with a paring chisel. Replace veneer with a diamond-shaped plug (see Fig. 1 and page 91). If cutting seems too drastic, disguise by graining (see page 116). This technique can also camouflage other surface blemishes.

Fig 1: diamond-shaped veneer replacement

VENEER REPAIRS

Veneering, or the art of laying thin, often precious, sheets of wood onto a solid timber base, ranks among the most fascinating aspects of furniture making. Used by the ancient Egyptians, and developed in Europe from the 16th century, it is a technique that allows for infinite possibilities and variations, including marquetry, parquetry and inlay. It is a practicable way of using rare, expensive or hard-to-work woods, exploiting their decorative qualities to a maximum: beautifully marked hardwood burrs, wild grained and brittle, and dramatically figured mahogany curl, both scarce and prohibitively expensive, achieve a new dimension when sliced into veneer and laid upon more banal woods.

The element of illusion implicit in veneered furniture has led to the common misconception that veneering is a cheap substitute for solid wood or a means of concealing poor construction. We can blame the Industrial Revolution for this unfortunate reputation – the emergence of a middle-income group and the enormous demand for factory-produced furniture led, inevitably, to indifferent workmanship, reflected in the diminishing quality of veneer. The invention of the veneer peeling machine in 1811, and the veneer cutting machine, also meant that

The exquisite and highly patterned figure of burr and butt walnut are used to great effect on this antique chest of drawers. Too rare and too structurally weak to be used as solid wood, burr and butt (see page 17) come into their own as a veneer.

veneers were now cut much thinner than the hand-sawn veneers of the preceding centuries, a point worth remembering in restoration.

For a truer perspective, take a look at museum pieces, particularly of the 17th and 18th centuries – you will be amazed by the craftsman's skill and ingenuity, and by the sheer beauty and variation of the woods.

Veneer is not, however, without drawbacks. With age, mistreatment or humidity, it will crack, chip, blister or lift. It has been calculated that, in restoration, it accounts for the most frequent repair work, after chairs. Repairs can vary from gluing small replacement inserts to laying whole sheets. Although the basic process is usually straightforward, great care must be taken in matching colour and figuring (see page 16). Remember that French polish or wax will darken your chosen colour.

HAMMER VENEERING

This is the traditional method of laying flat leaves of veneer by hand, without pressure or clamps: it is particularly suitable for the small workshop. A veneer hammer (bearing no resemblance to a conventional hammer) is used to press the veneer against the glued groundwork. To stop the ends of veneer cracking while you work, stick veneer tape across them (see page 27). This is also useful for joining pieces of veneer together, before laying them on the glue. The temperature in your workshop is very important: it should be over 20°C (68°F) and dust free.

EQUIPMENT

Household sponge / blunted paint knife / jack plane / toothing plane or old tenon saw / dusting cloth / large glue brush / iron / veneer hammer / lint-free cotton rag / veneer saw or craft knife / straight batten

METHOD
Preparation

1 It is essential that your surface is free from all dust and old glue. Sponge with hot water and a blunted paint knife.
2 Smooth with a jack plane to remove any irregularities or high spots on the surface (Fig. 1).

Fig.1: smoothing the surface

Fig. 2: scored surface

Keying

Holding the toothing plane (or old tenon saw) in one hand, and using the other hand to steady the front of it, move the plane randomly over the wood. The finely serrated cutting edge will score the wood and maximize the gluing surface (Fig. 2). Work the plane until the whole area is covered in small grooves and any remaining high spots are removed. Dust thoroughly.

Gluing

1 Prepare the hot pearl glue (see page 45). Beginners tend to make it too thick – for laying sheet veneer it should run off the brush without lumps or drops, rather like single cream.
2 Brush a thin, even layer of glue onto the prepared, keyed surface, in the direction of the grain (see page 90, Fig. 3), using a large glue brush The glue will cool and gel quite rapidly but do not worry: this allows you to position, and even re-position, the veneer without an immediate bond.

Fig. 3: brushing on the glue

Fig. 4: laying the veneer

Fig. 5: heating and hammering

Fig. 6: increasing the pressure

Placing the veneer

1 Dampen the underside of the veneer with a sponge.

2 Lay the veneer onto the glued surface (Fig. 4). Re-position until satisfied for fit.

Heating and hammering

If you are covering a sizeable surface, work it in sections, heating and hammering one section before starting the next. This will keep the glue at the right temperature.

1 Pre-heat the iron to a medium setting, and work slowly over the veneered surface, starting in the middle and using a circular motion. The cooled glue will gently melt and be drawn up into the pores of the veneer.

2 Still keeping the iron on the move, use the veneer hammer simultaneously to press down the veneer (Fig. 5). It has a double action – forcing out any remaining air and bedding the veneer deeper into the softened glue. Hold the hammer at an acute angle to the surface and work along the grain of the wood. (Working against the grain will 'stretch' the veneer, and later this will shrink, causing fit problems.)

3 Set the iron aside and increase the pressure on the hammer, using both hands to work over the surface (Fig. 6).

Cleaning and trimming

1 Remove any excess glue with a damp rag.

2 Trim off the surplus veneer, running a veneer saw (or craft knife) along a straight batten.

PATCHING VENEER

EQUIPMENT

Choose as appropriate: lint-free cotton rag / gent's saw / fretsaw / small glue brush / clamps / masking tape / low-angled block plane

METHOD

1 Dampen the piece you intend to use to check for colour – a simple way to emulate the effect of polish or wax on a finish. It should match the old veneer as closely as possible.

2 For best results, make a patch that is diamond shaped. It is impossible to match end grain with a square cut. The grain of the new piece should run in the same direction as the original. Cut out, using a gent's saw for straight edges and a fretsaw for wavy edges.

3 Glue, using hot pearl glue (see page 45). To clamp large areas, see Repairing Blisters (below). For small areas, use masking tape, but do not leave it on for more than 24 hours.

4 Thicker veneer may have to be levelled in order to match the surrounding area, using a low-angled block plane.

REPAIRING BLISTERS

EQUIPMENT

Choose as appropriate: craft knife / palette knife / electric iron / greaseproof paper / speed clamp / plywood blocks / small block / weights

METHOD

1 Slit the blister with the tip of a craft knife, making sure you follow the direction of the grain.

2 Insert hot pearl glue (see page 45) into both sides of the slit, using the tip of a palette knife (Fig. 1).

3 Preheat the iron, set at medium–low (synthetics), and run the tip of it along the mend.

4 Cover the mend with greaseproof paper, and speed clamp immediately (see page 47), 'sandwiching' the piece between two plywood blocks to distribute the pressure evenly (Fig. 2). Use a small block and weights if this is not possible.

Fig. 1: inserting glue

Fig. 2: clamping between blocks

VENEER REPAIRS

REPLACING STRINGING

From the 18th century, the edge detailing of cabinets was often finished off by inlaying a thin strip of veneer in a contrasting colour called stringing. As well as being decorative, this masked the joins where the main pieces of veneer met and provided protection for delicate corners. Since these strips are usually made from a different species of wood than the main veneer, they are prone to different expansion and contraction stresses and tend to be the first pieces to fall off. Stringing is relatively easy to replace; we give full details in one of our projects (see page 153). Available ready made from specialist suppliers, it can be found in a variety of woods and dimensions.

Fig. 1: 'clamping' the stringing

REPLACING MISSING INLAY

EQUIPMENT **Acetate / felt-tip pen / craft knife / fretsaw / small glue brush / electric iron / greaseproof paper / clamps**

METHOD **1** Lay a sheet of acetate over the empty recess and trace the shape with a felt-tip pen. Cut out with a craft knife.
2 Tape the template onto replacement veneer, matching the grain direction.
3 Cut with a fretsaw (Fig. 1), glue (see page 45) and clamp (page 91, Blisters).

Fig. 1: cutting the new inlay

CLAMPING CURVED VENEER

EQUIPMENT **2 old pillowcases / fine, dry sand / twine / small glue brush / lint-free cotton rag / greaseproof paper / plywood board / deep-throat G-clamps**

METHOD **1** Preheat the oven to 170°C (325°C, Gas Mark 3).
2 Fill one pillowcase with sand, place it inside another for added security and tightly bind each one with twine.
3 Switch off the oven, place the sandbag inside it and leave to warm gently for 30 minutes while you glue and lay the replacement piece (see page 45).
4 Squeeze out all the excess glue, wipe clean with rag, and lay greaseproof paper on the repair.

5 Place the heated sandbag on top of the glued veneer, moulding it around the curved surface, and then compress it with the board. Secure with one or more deep-throat G-clamps (Fig. 1) and leave to dry (12 hours).

6 Remove the clamps and sandbag (Fig. 2), and finish as required to match the existing surface.

Fig. 1: clamping the repair

Fig. 2: Eames Chair before finish (page 168)

REMOVING AND REUSING OLD VENEER

In the restoration process, it is sometimes necessary to remove old veneer before replacing it. Whenever possible, conserve what you remove, although the surface will have been stripped of French polish or other finishes (see page 39) to allow the steaming process to penetrate the glue. This method will only work with hot pearl glue: modern glues are irreversible.

EQUIPMENT

Choose as appropriate: cotton cloth / iron / blunted paint knife / veneer tape / lint-free cotton rag / greaseproof paper / 2 flat boards / weights

METHOD

1 Pre-set an iron to medium hot. Place a wet cotton cloth on the stripped veneer and run the iron smoothly across it.

2 Take the cloth off and run the iron across the veneer again.

3 Alternate steps 1 and 2 in a constant motion. The steam should liquify the glue underneath.

4 When the veneer starts to lift, prise it loose, in the direction of the grain, using a blunted paint knife (Fig. 1). Hold with veneer tape if it starts to split.

5 Remove the old glue (see page 38).

6 Buckled veneer can be straightened. Dampen it and warm two flat boards with an iron. Protecting the veneer with greaseproof paper, sandwich it between the two warmed boards. Put weights on top and leave for 12 hours.

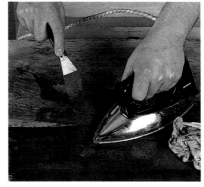

Fig. 1: prising off the veneer

FRENCH POLISHING

This most spectacular of traditional wood finishes first became popular in the 1820s and gradually replaced other finishes, such as wax, oil or resin varnishes. It is made by applying successive coats of shellac (see page 33), dissolved in alcohol, onto the prepared surface: the polish is skilfully worked into the wood rather than merely laid on top like paint. This 'fusion' between the wood and the polish creates a hard, mirror-like surface and an exceptionally deep, yet transparent lustre.

By the mid-19th century French polishing was in such demand that itinerant polishers would be employed for months on end in the grander houses, polishing every stick of furniture and even doors and window frames! Unfortunately many 18th-century and earlier pieces had their original finish replaced with French polish, giving rise to a certain confusion about the exact nature of wood finishes pre-1820.

French polishing requires few tools and minimal financial outlay. It does, however, demand patient practice to achieve that 'grand-piano' effect. Although best suited to mahogany and other exotic hardwoods, walnut, sycamore and even stained pine can be enhanced in this way.

Work in a clean, dust-free space. The temperature should be 18°C (64°F) or more; humidity can result in an opaque finish. Position your work against the light to see the polishing clearly. Practise first on plywood. Practise rubber-making too – it is vitally important. You can make French polish using solid shellac, but we recommend proprietary shellac polish as the basis of your polishes. It is impractical to make less than the quantities given, but they have a shelf life of 6 months.

POLISHING HARDWOODS

MATERIALS

Quantity for an area 1m²
French polishes ▶ 150ml transparent proprietary shellac polish (see page 33) / 50ml methylated spirits
Bodying up ▶ 2tsp raw linseed oil
Spiriting off ▶ 50ml methylated spirits
Cutting the shine (optional) ▶ 50ml clear proprietary beeswax

EQUIPMENT

2 glass bottles / 2 labels / 2 corks / craft knife / pure cotton wadding / 2 washed, white linen squares (25 x 25cm), torn to avoid loose threads / spirit-resistant vinyl gloves / clean wood offcut / plywood practice board / 2 airtight, wide-necked glass jars / 180-grade silicone-carbide paper / lint-free cotton rags / (optional) superfine wirewool (grade 0000)

METHOD
Preparing the French polishes

1 Pour 100ml transparent shellac polish into one of the bottles and label 'pure polish'.
2 Pour 50ml methylated spirits and 50ml transparent shellac polish into the other bottle, labelling '50/50 polish'.
3 Using a craft knife, cut a thin wedge from each cork to make drop-by-drop stoppers.

Making a rubber

1 Remove any paper backing and tease a handful of pure cotton wadding roughly into a pear shape. This is known as the 'fad'. Place it in the middle of a washed linen square. Taking one of the lower corners of the square (Fig. 1), fold the linen diagonally over the fad to join the opposite corner.

2 Repeat with the other corner to form a triangle (Fig. 2).

3 Pull the linen taut and smooth at the apex of the triangle, gathering up and twisting any surplus cloth and making sure no wadding escapes (Fig. 3). This creates the 'rubber', which should resemble a white mouse with a short, twisted tail.

4 Hold it firmly with the tail twisted in the palm of your hand and fingertips slightly extended. Check there are no bumps or wrinkles on the pad to spoil a smooth finish (Fig. 4).

Fig. 1: first fold

Fig. 2: second fold

Fig. 3: smoothing

Fig. 4: holding the rubber

Charging the rubber

1 Holding the rubber in one hand, open the linen covering and pour pure polish liberally onto the fad (Fig. 5). Think of the 'tail' as a screw top you twist open occasionally to add polish.

2 Re-wrap the fad as before.

3 Squeeze out any excess polish by pressing the rubber onto a wood offcut: it should 'sweat', not ooze. This also spreads polish evenly in the rubber.

Fig. 5: charging

Fadding

1 Spread an even film of polish over the entire surface with the charged rubber, alternating long, firm strokes applied across the grain and then along it. Press down firmly to force the polish into the pores, thus sealing the surface (Fig. 6). Avoid jerky movements and do not raise or lower the rubber vertically – it helps to think of an aeroplane taking off. When the rubber feels dry, recharge it with a few drops of polish but keep the movement constant and even. Pauses will cause polish to build up in ridges called 'whips'.

2 Repeat the process three or four times, making sure the whole surface is covered each time. Leave to dry (24 hours), storing the rubber in one of the airtight jars. Make a rule of storing the rubber in the closed jar whenever you are not using it – even during a short coffee-break. If left uncovered, the alcohol will evaporate and the rubber hardens. Stored properly, it will last for 6 months.

Denibbing

The surface, although dry, will still be rough at this stage. Rub down lightly with the silicone-carbide paper, pressing it flat and moving in the direction of the grain (Fig. 7). Dust thoroughly with a dampened cotton rag.

Polishing movements

fadding

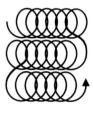

bodying up

Fig. 6: fadding

Fig. 7: denibbing

Bodying up

1 Recharge the rubber with pure polish and apply again to the whole surface, using straight strokes along and then across the grain. Repeat once or twice more.

2 Begin making circles approx. 10cm in diameter, each one overlapping the last, to cover the entire surface a further two or three times.

3 Alternate the circles with figures-of-eight in a continuous, gliding movement in the direction of the grain – remember the aeroplane – gradually increasing the pressure. A glossy sheen now begins to build up. The polish will dry more rapidly at this stage so the rubber needs extra lubrication. Dip a finger into the linseed oil and dab it directly onto the rubber (Fig. 8). Use sparingly – just enough to keep the

Fig. 8: adding linseed oil

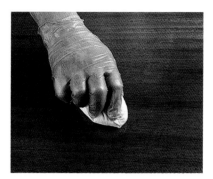

Fig. 9: using 50/50 polish

rubber on the move. The polish may also have a tendency to streak at this point, due to pressure on the still soft preceding coats or to too much polish. Stop for 1 hour – the streaks will not necessarily disappear but they will at least be stabilized.

4 Now begin using the 50/50 polish: this will speed up the drying and hardening process. Continue the circles and figures-of-eight (Fig. 9), recharging with polish as necessary. You can leave the surface to dry overnight between complete 'circuits'. Stop when the surface is perfectly smooth and glossy – with practice you will be able to judge the moment exactly. Leave for 24 hours.

Spiriting off

1 Make a second rubber, which must be kept specifically for this job.

2 Charge with methylated spirits and glide over the surface, working across and along the grain in circles and figures-of-eight, to remove any traces of oil and give the surface a high-gloss finish (Fig. 10). Leave to dry (1 week). Store the rubber in the other air-tight jar.

Fig. 10: spiriting off

Note French polish is easily marked by water and heat, and spilt alcohol will dissolve it, so it is wise to protect the surface with colourless proprietary beeswax (see page 122). To remedy marks and stains, see page 82.

CUTTING THE SHINE

The traditional, highly glossed look of French polishing is not always desirable in restoration: today taste leans towards a softer, more natural-looking sheen. To achieve this effect, wait a week after spiriting off and then apply clear beeswax with superfine wirewool (grade 0000), rubbed in a circular movement. The wax will also protect the finish.

REPAIRS AND SUBSTITUTIONS

Repairs It is sometimes possible – when repairing small areas of damage – to remove only the very top layer of French polish. First, use white spirit and superfine wirewool (grade 0000) to strip all traces of wax, and then apply very light pressure with a lint-free rag moistened with methylated spirits to soften and remove the top layer. When absolutely dry, wipe with a rag just moistened with white spirit. Allow to dry again. Now follow the instructions for Bodying up, step 4 onwards (page 97), using a 50/50 polish (see pages 33 and 94) and a rubber (see page 95). The old polish will amalgamate with the new.

Substitutions Effecting small repairs on modern finishes can present problems. Cellulose lacquers, introduced in the 1930s, and present-day synthetic lacquers have often been applied with industrial sprays and it is difficult or uneconomic to replicate the exact effect (on particularly matt surfaces) in a home workshop. Although proprietary shellac polish (see page 33) does not have the same strength or durability as these finishes, it imitates them successfully when applied to small areas, and has the advantage of being easily reversible.

Make sure the old surface surrounding the new insert is absolutely clean and wax free. Cut with superfine wirewool (grade 0000). Working with a circular movement in the direction of the grain to mimic the original surface, apply two coats of shellac to the new surface, using a rubber (see page 95), avoiding any build-up on the old surface, and allowing 3 hours' drying time between coats. Leave to dry (1 week), storing the rubber in an airtight jar.

SHELLAC POLISH AS VARNISH

Paintwork and gilding Shellac polish has traditionally been used as a varnish for paintwork and for gilding but this is not without complications as it can darken considerably and also crack. However, for furniture painted with oil- and water-based paints (not acrylics) it has a limited but successful role as a protection, and one that is easily removable. Use transparent or white proprietary shellac polish (see page 33), both of which are less likely to discolour. Apply one coat with a camel mop for a thicker effect or a rubber (see page 95) for a thinner effect and leave to dry (3 days). This is not suitable for pale colours or fine painted furniture: seek expert advice.

Metal fittings Clear shellac polish seals metal too. Apply one coat with a camel mop and leave to dry (2–3 hours).

The major disadvantage of a French polish finish is that it is easily marked by heat and moisture. On this little oval table the beauty of the walnut burr veneer top had quite disappeared after a lifetime of unsteady wine glasses and stray coffee cups. The French polish had deteriorated to such an extent that we had no choice but to strip the area (see page 39) and replace the finish. This presented a very real dilemma. The table was 18th century, in a modest neoclassical style, and would originally have had an oil varnish and wax finish, but reinstating this finish would have meant stripping the whole piece and losing precious patina. We opted to French polish the top, using as our base a transparent shellac polish to avoid obscuring the figuring. Polish tends to be unevenly absorbed by butts and burls (see page 17) so we applied polish sparingly when bodying up, taking extra care to push it into the grain. We then cut the shine to blend new polish and old, and the final result was very pleasing.

WORKING WITH GESSO

For thousands of years craftsmen have coated wood with layers of gesso – a substance generally made from a blend of animal glue and whiting (calcium carbonate) – to create a silky-smooth yet resilient foundation for the application of gold leaf or paint. Thicker layers were also worked to simulate carved wood: picture frames are an excellent example. A treatise written by Cennino Cennini in the 15th century remains to this day a standard reference when making gesso: now, as then, the formula for success lies in a keen awareness of heating and mixing procedures, careful observation of humidity levels, and an almost intuitive sense of timing. Once mastered, you will find this technique invaluable for all sorts of repairs.

Intricately carved wood on an 18th-century console: whether the gesso was once gilded or painted is now hard to tell. Gesso, simply polished with wax, is sometimes used as a final finish.

The drying process is very important. Ideally gesso should be applied in an unheated space, such as a garage or cellar. Do not be tempted to speed the process by any form of artificial heating. For this reason drying times can vary considerably, depending on the climate. Any metal nails and fastenings you intend to cover should be protected with small pieces of aluminium foil or they will discolour the gesso and eventually break it down. It is impractical to make up less than the quantities given here – inevitably there is a certain amount of wastage involved in the process of application. Always make more than you think you need so as to avoid running out in the middle of a job: excess gesso and size can be stored for a week in the fridge or 3 months in the freezer. Be sure to label it clearly.

FOUNDATION FOR PAINT OR GILDING

INGREDIENTS

Quantity for 250ml gesso
Mixing the size (approx. 170ml) ▶ 10g rabbit-skin glue granules / water to cover (approx. 170ml) / hot water to dilute (if required)
Priming with size ▶ 1tsp (rounded) artists' quality whiting
Mixing the gesso ▶ approx. 260g artists' whiting (see Priming, page 101)

EQUIPMENT

Slow cooker (see page 46) or heatproof bowl and saucepan / wooden spoon / jug / teaspoon / gesso brush / covered plastic container for storing gesso / tablespoon / fine sieve / linen cloth for smoothing / smooth wood offcut / dental scraper for detail, if required

METHOD
Mixing the size

1 Placing the glue granules in the slow cooker (or heatproof bowl), pour over them just enough cold water to cover and leave to soak overnight.
2 Warm the fluffy, swollen glue granules in the slow cooker (Fig. 1) or over water barely simmering in the saucepan. Stir

from time to time with the wooden spoon until you achieve a thick, smooth liquid (Fig. 2). Do not allow to boil or overheat. (If this happens at any stage in the process, you must throw the mixture away and start again.)

3 When cooled to room temperature, press a forefinger into the mixture to test for strength. Size should have a soft, jelly-like consistency and break apart with rough edges: a springy resistance or smooth break indicates that there is too much glue in the mix. Dilute with hot water, stir, cool, and repeat the test until satisfied.

Fig. 1: warming the soaked granules   **Fig. 2: liquid glue**

Priming with size

1 Warm the size again, pour a quarter of it (just over 40ml) into the jug and slide in 1 rounded teaspoon artists' whiting. Let it sink into the solution; then stir gently but thoroughly. This gives the size a milky appearance, making it much easier to see your brush strokes and therefore to achieve the even coverage that helps gesso adhere well.

2 Brush thinly and evenly onto the prepared surface (see page 40). If air bubbles form, rub them out gently with your forefinger. Leave to dry (minimum 48 hours).

3 Store the remaining cooled size in the covered plastic container in the fridge for no more than a week. Particularly absorbent or coarse-grained wood will need a second coat.

Mixing the gesso

You should aim to complete this and the following stage in one day so an early morning start is advisable.

1 Re-heat the remaining size in the slow cooker (or bowl) as before.

2 Stir in, a tablespoon at a time, the rest of the artists' whiting, as for Priming, step 1. The consistency should be that of smooth single cream (Fig. 3).

3 Strain the mixture through the fine sieve and leave to stand (30 mintues).

Fig. 3: consistency of gesso

WORKING WITH GESSO

Applying the gesso

1 Brush on an even coat of warm gesso. Be constantly alert for any bubbles, rubbing them out as before. Even the tiniest pin-prick can spoil the final smooth surface.

2 When the first coat is just dry to the touch (1–2 hours), brush on a second coat, applying it at right angles to the first to avoid any build up of brush marks. For difficult angles and carved details, hold the brush vertically and apply the gesso with a stippling (or dabbing) movement.

3 When again just dry, smooth down with the damp linen cloth – you may need to rinse it occasionally.

4 Repeat steps 1 and 2 for a total of 6–8 coats (Fig. 4), omitting further smoothing with the linen cloth. It is important to keep the gesso fluid. If necessary, warm it occasionally in the slow cooker or bowl but remember that overheating creates air bubbles.

5 Leave the surface to harden (2 days before gilding, 6 days before painting).

Fig. 4: applying gesso

Fig. 5: polishing with an offcut

Wet polishing

To create the smooth, flat surface you need for painting and gilding, smooth again with the (clean) linen cloth, evenly dampened with water and wrapped around a piece of suitably contoured wood (Fig. 5). This method replaces sandpaper, which would create dust. For corners and crevices, wrap the cloth around your forefinger. Smooth and sharpen intricate carvings with a dental scraper.

PATCHING WITH GESSO

Provided the solution is not too strong, new gesso has the ability to amalgamate with old gesso. This is particularly useful when patching chipped or missing pieces on painted and gilded surfaces. Apply the new gesso in layers as described above. The last coat should stand just proud of the existing surface. Leave to dry and then wet polish and level with a linen cloth. You must avoid touching surrounding water-based paintwork or gilding, but resist the temptation to mask – masking creates straight lines that cannot be blended with the old surfaces and risks damage to gilding.

Since furthest antiquity, craftsmen have applied tissue-thin sheets of beaten gold to all kinds of objects, magically transforming banal woods and base metals with this most glamorous yet durable of surface finishes. Originally restricted to a closed circle of initiates whose tools and techniques remained substantially unchanged for centuries, the art of gilding still retains its tantalizing, mysterious hint of alchemy in the face of modern-day technology. For restoration purposes, both water gilding and oil gilding are useful: we describe both techniques.

WATER GILDING

Nothing can quite match the exquisite brilliance of water gilding. Careful preparation and patiently acquired skills are required to 'float' gossamer-thin gold leaf over a gesso and bole surface, and then to burnish the piece for an extra-smooth shine. It is principally these techniques that differentiate water gilding from other gilding, and give it a very special luminosity.

MATERIALS

Quantity for an area 1m^2
Applying the size/bole ▶ 170ml size (see page 100, Mixing the size, reserving 1tbsp for Applying the leaf) / 1tbsp yellow bole / 2tbsp red bole
Applying the leaf ▶ 1tbsp size (see above) / 400ml water / 100ml clear or isopropyl alcohol / $^1/_2$tbsp methylated spirits / 150 leaves gold leaf

EQUIPMENT

Tablespoon / 2 containers for size/bole / slow cooker or heatproof bowl and saucepan / white-bristled brush / camel mop / 500-grade aluminium oxide paper / stiff shoe brush / gilder's knife / cottonwool / gilder's cushion / gilder's tip / squirrel mop / cotton gloves (optional) / agate burnisher

METHOD
Applying the size/bole

1 The surface must be primed with size, gessoed and wet polished for an impeccably smooth surface (see page 100). Any defect will become much more obvious once gilded.
2 Place 1 tablespoon yellow bole in one of the containers and gradually stir in 5 tablespoons size warmed in the slow cooker (or heatproof bowl and saucepan), mixing the bole/size solution to the consistency of milk.
3 Dust the surface of the piece with the white-bristled brush and apply the size/bole at once, using the camel mop. Coat evenly and smoothly, eliminating air bubbles with a fingertip. Gesso is very absorbent so, if necessary, apply a second coat after 1 hour. Leave to dry (12 hours).
4 Warm 6 tablespoons size and stir into 2 tablespoons red bole in the second container, mixing to a thin cream.
5 Apply two or three coats over the yellow bole, allowing each one to become touch-dry before applying the next (approx. 1 hour). Leave to harden (24 hours).

6 Sand the surface gently with the aluminium oxide paper to remove any imperfections and then dust as before.

7 Buff vigorously to a lustrous red sheen, using the (clean) shoe brush. Dust again.

Applying the leaf

1 To make 'gilding water', warm 1 tablespoon size in the slow cooker (or heatproof bowl), gradually add the water, stirring well, and cool; then add the alcohol, stirring again.

2 Place the piece on a slight slope to ensure the liquid will not 'puddle' but form a thin film – this is essential if the gold leaf is to bond successfully – and, using the camel mop, brush the gilding water generously over a small area (no more than 10–15 cm² at a time).

3 Wipe the gilder's knife with a cottonwool pad moistened with methylated spirits to degrease it. Using only the knife (not your fingers!), slide a leaf onto the gilder's cushion and reposition until reasonably flat. Then breathe just once directly down onto it to remove any wrinkles.

4 Use the knife to cut the leaf to size, if required.

5 Run the end of the gilder's tip across the back of your neck, just under the hair-line. (The minute quantity of body oils collected in this way acts as an excellent natural adhesive so do not wash your hair just before gilding!) Using the tip, pick up the gold leaf (Fig. 1) and lay it down on the wet surface. The water will attract it instantly like a magnet so judge the angle at which you are laying the leaf carefully. Leave for 1–2 minutes.

Fig. 1: using a gilder's tip

6 Press the leaf gently but firmly with a cottonwool pad to ensure it is secure and to remove any bubbles. Use the squirrel mop to tap down small areas.

7 Dampening small areas at a time, repeat steps 3–6 as required to gild the entire surface. To avoid watermarks, lay each leaf to cover slightly more than the dampened area with as little overlap on surrounding leaf as possible. In time, this process can become an almost continuous movement.

Faulting

Even the most accomplished gilder will find a few water spots or areas of exposed bole when finished.

1 Dampen the area and its immediate surroundings with gilding water, apply a generous piece of leaf, and breathe on it heavily to amalgamate surfaces not touched with water.

2 Apply light pressure with a cottonwool pad.

Burnishing

This process will shine, smooth and 'stretch' the gold over the bole like a second skin. It also secures loose gold and obscures the joins. The interval between gilding and burnishing depends upon the ambient temperature and humidity: it can vary between 2 hours and 2 days but it is always better to err on the side of a too dry surface than one that is too damp. A dry surface will emit a sharp 'click' when tapped with the burnisher, and a dull sound if still too damp. Before you begin, ensure that your agate is clean, dry and perfectly smooth, and wear cotton gloves when burnishing small items to avoid damage from hot hands.

Below: Water and oil gilding. Note the much flatter, duller appearance of oil gilding, and the more effective antiquing on water gilding. Loose gold leaf was used on the water-gilded table. For the oil-gilded table, we used loose gold leaf on the details but transfer leaf on the level surfaces.

Fig. 2: using a burnisher

1 Run the agate burnisher very gently all over the gilding, using a series of small, circular movements (Fig. 2).

2 Increase the pressure gradually for each successive stroke. Make sure you give the whole piece the same even degree of burnish, unless there are areas you want to leave matt for an attractive contrast. Leave for 24 hours before patinating or antiquing (see page 107).

❶ WATER GILDING
a yellow bole
b red bole
c red bole, polished
d loose gold leaf, burnished
e loose gold leaf, antiqued

❷ OIL GILDING
a yellow bole
b red bole
c shellac on bole
d loose gold leaf
e transfer leaf
f transfer leaf, antiqued
g loose leaf, antiqued

Water and oil gilding can be combined on the same piece to great effect. On this 19th-century French mirror water gilding on the carved and incised details contrasts handsomely with the matt surfaces of oil gilding.

OIL GILDING

This is a simpler, less fragile finish than water gilding. It cannot be burnished, however, and therefore does not achieve the same high-voltage brilliance. A gesso foundation is not vital but gives a better surface. Transfer gold leaf (see page 35) can be used instead of loose leaf on flat surfaces, which also simplifies the process.

MATERIALS

Size/bole ▶ see Water gilding, omitting 1tbsp size reserved for the leaf
Shellac ▶ 150ml transparent proprietary shellac polish (see page 33)
Gold size ▶ 4–5tbsp gold size
Gilding ▶ See Water gilding or substitute transfer leaf on flat areas

EQUIPMENT

Tablespoon / slow cooker or heatproof bowl and saucepan / 2 containers for size/bole / white-bristled brush / camel mop / 500-grade aluminium oxide paper / stiff shoe brush / wood offcut / gesso brush / cottonwool For loose leaf only: gilder's knife / gilder's cushion / gilder's tip

METHOD
Size/bole

See Water gilding (page 103). After polishing to a sheen with the stiff shoe brush, allow the surface to dry (48 hours).

Shellac

Using the camel mop, apply two thin coats of shellac to the piece and the offcut, leaving 24 hours for each coat to dry.

Gold size

Brush a very thin coat of gold size onto the piece and offcut with a gesso brush kept solely for this purpose. Beginners should use gold size which allows for 12 hours' drying time. Beware of dust, and cover if necessary. Since '12 hours' is approximate, depending on climatic conditions, it is important to test progress from time to time. Touch the wood offcut with your forefinger: when it feels tacky but no fingerprint can be seen, it is time to gild.

Gilding Transfer gold can be laid directly onto flat surfaces. For moulded or carved areas, apply loose leaf as in water gilding, omitting the 'gilding water'. Press with cottonwool to ensure adhesion. Leave for 1 week before antiquing or patinating.

ANTIQUING AND PATINATING

Antiquing Water gilding: very gently distress with superfine wirewool (grade 0000) to remove tiny fragments of gold leaf, exposing the bole beneath. Reburnish if you wish. Oil gilding: rub with linen rag, moistened with white spirit.

Patinating This is a useful technique for blending old gilding with new and can be used for both water and oil gilding. Dilute 1 tablespoon size with 50ml water, add 1 tablespoon rottenstone (if available, see page 110) and stir well. If possible, add dirt or dust collected from the piece being restored. Brush on with a camel mop, especially around cracks and crevices. Leave to dry (1 hour).

Below: Clay or Armenian bole, as it was first known, has three functions: to smooth out any irregularities in gessoed surfaces, subtly to enrich the colour of gilding and to enhance any areas where the gold leaf is missing.

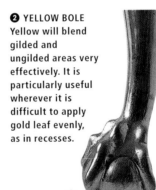

❶ RED BOLE
Generally applied over yellow, red is the colour usually associated with gilding. It brings a rich glow to burnished, worn or distressed surfaces.

❷ YELLOW BOLE
Yellow will blend gilded and ungilded areas very effectively. It is particularly useful wherever it is difficult to apply gold leaf evenly, as in recesses.

❸ GREY BOLE
Dark grey bole was much prized during the 17th century and was revived again during the Art Deco period.

❹ BROWN BOLE
Sometimes colour is determined by availability. Here brown is used for a 'period feel' – anything from 17th-century baroque to 19th-century opulence.

AGED PAINT

The 18th-century vogue for pale, painted surfaces – the chalky whites, gentle blue-greys and rich, powdery creams we associate with French and Swedish furniture of the Louis Quinze and Louis Seize periods – is still with us today as an attractive means of camouflaging inexpensive woods and, in some instances, hiding poor workmanship.

Quick, modern methods of painting directly onto primed wood can, however, never equal the subtly precious quality achieved by the traditional techniques of building up and smoothing down layers of gesso to give an impeccable surface and sense of 'depth' to the final paint finish. In restoration this method is useful when matching traditionally painted pieces or replacing parts.

The water-based, glue tempera paint recipe given here is distressed for an antique look, but for a fuller effect you must first lay down several layers of gesso (see page 100). The final stage – applying coloured or antiquing wax over the finish – simulates the patina of time; using this technique, paint colours can be subtly altered so that blue turns greyish and green khaki. Care should be taken not to overdo the effect, especially on carved pieces, because it can end up looking very 'repro'. However, it has the advantage of being reversible.

BASIC RECIPE – SWEDISH BLUE

MATERIALS

Quantity for an area 1m^2
For gesso primer see page 100.
Base coat ▶ 100ml gesso (see page 100) / 100ml rabbit-skin glue size (page 100) / 50ml water / artists' gouache colours: 1 dash lamp black, 1 dash yellow ochre, 1 dash raw sienna
Second coat ▶ 100ml gesso / 100ml rabbit-skin glue size / 50ml water / artists' gouache colours: 1 dash lamp black, 1 dot Prussian blue, (optional) 1 dot raw umber
Antiquing wax ▶ 50ml colourless proprietary beeswax / 1–1½tsp raw umber artists' powder pigment / ½tsp rottenstone or lamp black artists' powder pigment / ½tsp white spirit (for detail work, as required)

EQUIPMENT

For gesso primer see page 100.
Heatproof bowl and saucepan for warming size, glue tempera paint and wax / 2 covered containers for mixing glue tempera paint / 2 saucers / 25mm household paint brush / 2 sheets white paper to test colour / washed linen rag / mask / stiff shoe brush / lint-free cotton rags

METHOD
Base coats

1 Placing the prepared gesso and warm rabbit-skin glue size in one of the containers, mix thoroughly and then add the water (a little at a time), stirring again. You are aiming for a consistency somewhere between milk and single cream.
2 Using one of the saucers as a palette, mix the gouache colours, adding a little water to dilute and stirring well.

3 Stir the colour-mix into the gesso/size solution. When cold, test for consistency with your finger. Glue tempera paint should wobble, but not feel too rubbery. If it is still runny, you have probably added too much water. Some of the cheaper gouache colours contain a high proportion of extender (to cut down on the amount of pigment they use) and this has a tendency to curdle the gesso/size solution. If it happens, you have no option but to start again, using a different brand.

4 Test the colour on a piece of white paper and leave to dry (2–4 hours), storing the solution (covered) in the fridge: size can go 'off'. The test piece will lighten considerably to a colour best described as 'taupe'. This is the time to adjust the tone if required, adding diluted colour, and retesting.

5 Warm over hot water and then brush liberally and unevenly onto the gessoed surface. A certain amount of texture heightens the aged effect. Leave to dry (2–4 hours).

Second coat

1 Using the same method, tint a fresh quantity of the gesso/size solution with the mixed and diluted Prussian blue and lamp black. Prussian blue is a very, very strong colour so use sparingly!

2 Test run the second coat on another piece of paper. Add a little more lamp black for a more pronounced blue-grey effect. If it still looks 'new', add raw umber to cut the glare.

3 Brush on the second coat, applying the paint more lightly than the base coat. Allow to dry fully (24 hours).

Distressing

Rub a washed linen rag, moistened with water, firmly over the surface, using circular movements, to emphasize raised

❶ SWEDISH BLUE The basic recipe : this reversible technique looks 'authentic' both on period pieces and on more recent, junk-shop finds.

❷ FRENCH CREAM Another period colour: here two coats of very similar colour are used, the first being just a little darker than the second. Test the combination on paper before you begin. Gouache colours: zinc white, raw umber, yellow ochre and lamp black (see page 133).

details and areas subject to constant wear. In this way you will cut through the upper layer of paint, exposing some of the base coat beneath. When distressed to match the existing piece, leave to dry (24 hours).

Antiquing wax

ALWAYS WEAR A MASK WHEN USING POWDER PIGMENTS.

1 Place the beeswax in the heatproof bowl over a saucepan of hot water and soften very gently.

2 Add the powder pigment(s) and rottenstone. Rottenstone is a bulking agent, often hard to find, used by jewellers and watch makers for polishing. Substitute lamp black powder pigment if unavailable. This is also the time to add dust collected when cleaning the piece. Stir and allow to cool.

3 Test in an inconspicuous place, applying with the shoe brush. Allow to dry (1 hour). To lighten the colour, use more beeswax; darken with a little more powder pigment.

4 Apply the wax, building it up in recesses and details. If difficult, thin with white spirit and work in using the paint brush. Leave to dry (1 hour).

5 Gently buff with lint-free cotton rags.

ADAPTING FOR OIL-BASED PAINTED SURFACES

Although this is not strictly restoration and the result will not have the conviction that glue tempera paint on gesso brings, you can adapt this Aged Paint technique for use on surfaces ready painted with oil-based paints, such as we found on the Dressing Table (see page 162). Use eggshell paint tinted with artists' oil colours, as described on page 164. Distress with wet-and-dry sandpaper and medium wirewool (grade 0).

'SWEDISH' STOOL

Long, low stools are a useful addition to period furnishings: they provide not only additional seating but are also an elegant alternative to the modern-day coffee table, which can look out of place in an antique setting. This one was found, unpainted, in an auction; it had probably formed the leg-rest of an 18th-century *duchesse-brisée* or day-bed. Although the cabriole legs were nicely carved in

fruitwood, the cross-rails had been replaced with an exotic hardwood stained in a failed attempt to colour match. Traces of paint on the underside and open galleries left by woodworm indicated that the piece had been originally painted – worms do not differentiate between paint and wood so if a piece has been stripped of paint any wormholes will run in open channels along the surface.

After treatment for woodworm (see page 36), the piece was stripped of its modern varnish (see page 39) and then repainted, distressed and waxed using the Aged Paint technique. The subtle choice of colour – Swedish Blue – was dictated by the room in which the stool would be placed: plain pine floors, a beautiful blue-and-white ceramic stove and dove-grey panelling all evoked the sophisticated simplicity of a Scandinavian interior. The final waxing gave the distressed paint just the right patina, and an upholstered stuff-over seat (see page 72) in a pale linen check completed the understated effect.

STAINING

In restoration the subtle art of staining is now principally used when matching new wood with old, for example, when replacing mouldings or repairing inlay. A good restorer will never try to change the natural colour of original, old wood and alter years of irreplaceable patina. However, staining has also traditionally been used for enhancing or transforming blander woods, such as cherry, beech or gaboon, to give a richer, more interesting aspect. In either case, stain must be protected with a wax or French polish finish (see pages 122 and 94).

Many types of ready-made stain are available, but none is entirely problem-free. For example, water- and spirit-based aniline dyes, although offering a good colour range, fade rapidly. Perfect colour-matches are rare too – 'medium oak' is unlikely to correspond to *your* piece of medium oak. Here we give advice on matching and the methods of staining we find most effective. Do remember when staining replacement pieces for inlay that they should be stained *before* being glued into place to avoid colour seepage.

MATCHING AN EXISTING STAIN

Successful staining requires close examination of the wood you wish to match or imitate and careful experimentation with colour mixes. Use a few same-wood scraps as a trial palette before the final staining: when fully dry, results can be surprising. Always aim for a lighter rather than darker tone: obviously, it is more difficult to lighten up than darken down. Once your stain has dried, damp it down with a moistened rag – this simple trick will give a helpful indication of what the surface is likely to look like after its eventual wax or French polish finish.

To achieve an even effect and avoid streaking, it is always preferable to apply two thin coats of stain, working in the direction of the grain, rather than one thick one. Allow the first coat to dry completely before applying the second coat. You may find that the colour has changed quite radically once dry so be prepared to modify the second coat by either strengthening or diluting the initial colour.

USING VANDYKE BROWN CRYSTALS

This method can be recommended as a general stain for small replacements on antique furniture since it imitates aged wood very passably and gives good results for oak, mahogany and walnut. If tinting oak, omit the ammonia because it will turn the wood an unattractive grey/brown. Like all water-based stains, it will raise the grain and require subsequent sanding. The proportions given can be diluted with more or less water as required – this stain can vary from palest honey, through warm chestnut, to almost black.

MATERIALS	Quantity for an medium-brown stain on an area 12m²
	60g vandyke brown crystals / 500ml warm water / 1tbsp household ammonia (not for oak, see opposite)

EQUIPMENT	Newspaper / lint-free cotton rags / 120-grade sandpaper / screwtop glass jar / mask / spirit-resistant vinyl gloves / 25mm household paint brush

METHOD

PROTECT YOUR WORK SPACE WITH NEWSPAPER.

1 Dampen the wood with a water-soaked rag to raise the grain. Allow to dry naturally and then gently rub down, using the sandpaper. Dust with damp rags.

2 Place the crystals in the glass jar and pour on the warm water, stirring continually until all the crystals are dissolved. Leave until cold.

3 FOR ALL BUT OAK: to aid penetration, add ammonia (taking care not to breathe the fumes) and stir again.

4 Wearing the mask and spirit-resistant gloves, brush the stain evenly in the direction of the grain.

5 Wipe off any excess stain with a damp rag in order not to leave any marks. Allow to dry (12 hours).

6 Gently sand the 'furry' surface of the grain (see page 112) and repeat the process. When dry, the surface will be ready for an appropriate finish.

❷ BICHROMATE OF POTASH
Like vandyke brown crystals, this stain is best kept for small replacement parts.

❶ VANDYKE BROWN CRYSTALS
Neutral plywood board was used for all six swatches. Compare the unstained top right corner, the stained, unpolished surface, and the stained and polished turned objects. End grain on a turned piece can darken the effect of a stain considerably.

USING BICHROMATE OF POTASH

These orange crystals, steeped in water, trigger a chemical reaction in the wood which causes the colour to darken. This method is used chiefly on mahogany and tannic-rich woods, such as oak, which it turns a rich, red brown. After the 1830s a great deal of factory-made furniture was stained in this way – the Victorians loved the highly-coloured effect, although to modern eyes it now seems rather florid. We use the crystals, sparingly, as an enhancer or for darkening replacement parts, but never as an overall stain.

STAINING

MATERIALS   Quantity for a red-brown stain on an area 12m²
2tbsp bichromate of potash / 500ml hot water

EQUIPMENT   See Vandyke Brown Crystals

METHOD   WEAR GLOVES AND MASK. PROTECT YOUR WORK SPACE WITH NEWSPAPER.
Follow the method used for Vandyke Brown Crystals, omitting step 3. Leave to dry (2–3 hours). The stain will look yellow at first but as the reaction takes effect it darkens to a reddish brown. If, when completely dry, yellow crystals have formed on the surface, wipe off with a damp rag.

USING NITRO STAINS

Oil based but ready-modified for use under all finishes ranging from cellulose varnish to shellac, these stains do not fade, have a transparent quality, are quick drying and easy to mix and match colourwise. They work very well for large areas and are easily controllable by the beginner. However, as with all manufactured stains, the basic colour-range looks unnatural and considerable experimentation is needed. The many shades of brown found in wood can vary from warm to cool, depending upon how much red or green they contain – warm colours lie at the red/yellow end of the colour spectrum, cool colours at the green/blue end. The professional will keep a stock of red, yellow, green and black to blend as required, but the amateur would be better advised to buy a basic selection of ready-mixed wood tones and experiment with colour mixing those on same-wood offcuts. A selection of mahogany, light and medium oak, and walnut – plus a bottle of nitro solvent, which lightens as it thins – would be a useful starting point.

The chart below offers guidelines for crossmixing ready-made nitro stains. Use a saucer to run trials, adding the nitro solvent (a little at a time) if thinning is needed and stirring well. Keep careful note of the proportions you use as you experiment so that you can mix the appropriate quantity once you have found your blend. Go easy on mahogany stains because the red in them tends to dominate. To emulate an aged effect, try laying down a vandyke brown stain as a base (see page 112) and then nitro stain as appropriate; never reverse the procedure. Blended nitro stains can be stored in a screwtop glass jar for up to 6 months.

MIXING NITRO STAINS

READY-MADE STAIN	DESCRIPTION	ADD TO COOL	ADD TO WARM
Mahogany	Rich red-brown	Walnut and Light Oak	
Medium Oak	Orangey-brown	Light Oak and Walnut	Mahogany and Light Oak
Light Oak	Light yellow-brown with greenish tone	Nitro solvent and Walnut	Nitro solvent and Medium Oak
Walnut	Greenish brown		Mahogany

STAINING

MATERIALS	Quantity for a medium-oak stain on an area 12m² 4tbsp white spirit or acetone (see step 1) / 400ml ready-mixed nitro stain, blended to required colour
EQUIPMENT	Newspaper / 120-grade sandpaper / spirit-resistant vinyl gloves / lint-free cotton rags / 25mm household paint brush (for detail)
METHOD	Protect your work space with newspaper.

1 Thoroughly sand the surface to be stained. Then, wearing the spirit-resistant gloves, dust with a clean rag moistened with white spirit or, in the case of resinous woods (such as pine, rosewood or cedar), acetone. This will effectively dissolve and remove any residual grease.

2 Again, wearing the gloves and using a clean rag, apply the blended stain evenly, liberally and in the direction of the grain. Use a 25mm household paint brush in hard-to-reach areas such as carved details.

3 Make sure that the pores are fully covered, but wipe off any excess stain with a rag: stain allowed to puddle on the surface will dry to form ugly rings. Leave to dry (6 hours).

4 Wipe over with a dry rag to remove any excess stain which might leach into the finish.

❸ MAHOGANY
❹ MEDIUM OAK
❺ LIGHT OAK
❻ WALNUT
NITRO STAINS
These four wood-effect, proprietary oil-based nitro stains can be the basis of a useful beginner's kit for large-scale work. A wide range of other colours is also available and can be intermixed to provide many subtle variations. Unobtainable woods can be 'mocked up' quite successfully in this way. We also use this stain to disguise unsightly scratches in leather work (see page 137, Finishing, step 6).

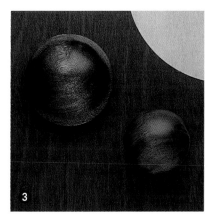

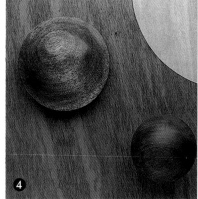

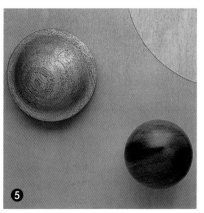

GRAINING

The ancient art of woodgraining or *faux bois* reached its apogee in the 19th century, when it became the fashion to paint doors, panelling and also furniture to imitate rarer forms of wood. In this way inexpensive, serviceable pine was magically transformed into walnut, mahogany, oak and an array of exotic woods. Properly done, the effect can vary from the solidly authentic to the wildly fanciful. Recent but transitory vogues for stripped-pine furniture often removed splendid examples of 18th- and 19th-century *faux bois*; reinstating the original decoration can create a more authentic and interesting piece. In restoration *faux bois* is also useful for replacement parts of highly figured woods such as walnut and rosewood. Although a specialized skill, amateurs can achieve results with experimentation and tenacity. The final wood colour depends upon the colour of the eggshell base coat and of the wash. Try a variety of earth colours for different effects. We recommend the brushes listed below as a good range for the beginner.

BASIC RECIPE – WALNUT

MATERIALS

Quantity for an area 2m²
Base coats ▶ 150ml oil-based orange-yellow eggshell paint (2 coats)
Wash coat ▶ 1tbsp whiting / 1 dash raw umber artists' acrylic colour / 1tbsp water
Figuring ▶ artists' acrylic colours: 1 dash lamp black, 1 dash burnt sienna, 1 dash raw sienna, 1 dash raw umber / 1tbsp water (maximum)
Overgraining ▶ artists' oil colours: 1 dot lamp black, 1 dot burnt sienna, 1 dot raw sienna, 1 dash raw umber / 1tbsp linseed oil / 1tbsp turpentine

EQUIPMENT

40mm household paint brush / lint-free cotton rags / 3 plates for mixing wash coat and tints / 50mm flogging brush / no. 2 sable brush / 30mm spalter or 25mm varnish brush / clean linen cloth / 70mm white-bristled dusting brush

METHOD
Base coats

Apply two even coats of oil-based eggshell paint to the entire prepared surface (see page 40), using the household brush. Allow 12 hours' drying time between the coats and leave the second to dry completely (24 hours).

Wash coat

1 Rub the surface with a little whiting, applied and removed with lint-free rags, to de-grease it.
2 Place the acrylic colour on one of the plates and add the water (a little at a time), stirring to mix to a thin wash.
3 Apply the wash, using the household brush.
4 While still wet, tap the dry flogging brush lightly across the surface as if you were drumming. The aim is to create a speckled surface that simulates the underlying grain of most woods. Leave to dry (1–2 hours).

a

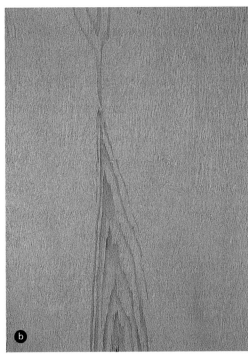

b

c

1

❶ WALNUT

a The thin wash of raw umber has been applied over the base colour and then flogged to speckle the surface.

b The heart grain is drawn in with the mid-brown tint using a sable brush: by first sketching in the basic shape and then blending away from the defining lines. A real wood sample or good picture reference is vital at this stage.

c With the paler glaze now applied on either side of the heart grain, the clean household paint brush is quickly dragged through it to render the straighter outer sections of grain, and a few heavier lines are added.

1 The finished sample with the rippled crossgrain characteristic of walnut: once the final oil-based glaze has been applied, a piece of soft, washed linen, stretched tautly between the hands, is dabbed gently over all but the heart grain.

GRAINING

Figuring

1 Place the acrylic colours on the second plate and mix well to create a mid-brown tint.

2 Draw in the heart grain (see swatch b on page 117), using the sable brush. Leave to dry (1–2 hours).

3 Dilute some of the remaining tint with water, stir and apply to the surrounding area with the spalter (or varnish brush).

4 Drag the dry household paint brush through the glaze to create the less distinct part of the grain. You may need to paint heavier lines on the outer grain, using the sable brush and the remaining undiluted glaze. Leave to dry (4 hours).

Overgraining

1 Place the oil colours on the third plate, pour on the linseed oil and stir well. Then add the turpentine (a little at a time), stirring continuously.

2 Apply the glaze evenly to the entire surface, using the household brush.

3 Holding the piece of linen taut between your hands, dab the glaze gently to create the crossgraining associated with walnut. Work over the entire surface, excluding the heart grain.

4 Lightly and carefully blend and unify the entire surface, using the dusting brush, and leave to dry (2–3 days).

Note This surface needs a protection that matches the finish on the piece. French polish will not be durable enough. When possible, apply one coat of semi-gloss polyurethane varnish, leave to dry (12 hours) and then wax (see page 122).

❷ MAHOGANY
The method is the same as for Walnut. Refer, if possible, to an existing sample. Substitute a light terracotta for the base coats, follow Walnut for the wash coat, and build up the flame figuring and the overgraining with burnt sienna and lamp black artists' acrylics and oils.

❸ OAK
This is a shorter process: on a light yellow base, the figuring is painted in with a sable brush, using raw sienna and raw umber artists' acrylics. No further work is necessary.

MARBLING

Antique tables, chests of drawers and consoles can sometimes be found for a fraction of their price because of missing, cracked or chipped marble tops. Cracked marble tops can be rejoined and chips remodelled using proprietary resin, but the cost of a completely new marble top can be prohibitive and its considerable weight will weaken antique joints. Learning to paint imitation marble is definitely worthwhile if you wish to maintain the decorative spirit of real marble. The art of marbling can be loosely separated into two techniques: dispersion, which uses a variety of solvents (alcohol, white spirit or water) to fracture or mottle the paint, or the careful drawing of the veining. The recipes given here demonstrate different aspects of these techniques. Always have an example of real marble or a photograph by you for reference, the larger the better as you need a clear idea of how the veining and 'pebbly' shapes would be disposed over an area of a similar size. Be sure to practise on sample board first – plywood is ideal.

VERDE-NERO MARBLE

It is important, if starting from scratch, to choose your marble colours carefully so that they harmonize with the existing wood or painted base. Here both marbling techniques are combined to achieve a sombre marble suitable for a dark wood base.

MATERIALS

Quantity for an area 2m²
Base coats ▶ 200ml black eggshell paint (2 coats)
Glaze coat ▶ artists' oil colours: 1 dash terre verde, 1 dash chrome green, 1 dash zinc white, 1 dash lamp black, 1 dot raw umber / 1tbsp linseed oil / 3 drops Japan dryers / 1tbsp white spirit
Adding veins ▶ artists' oil colours: 1 dash titanium white, 1 dot lamp black
Protective coats ▶ 200ml polyurethane varnish (4 coats)

EQUIPMENT

240-grade sandpaper / lint-free cotton rags / 40mm household paint brush / 2 plates for mixing / thin plastic shopping bag / 70mm soft, white-bristled dusting brush / round sable brush / 40mm varnish brush

METHOD
Base coats

1 To the thoroughly prepared (see page 40), sanded and dusted surface, apply one coat of eggshell with the household paint brush and leave to dry (24 hours).
2 Sand lightly and dust thoroughly with damp rags.
3 Apply a second coat of eggshell, leave to dry (2 days), and then sand and dust again. It is essential that the surface is absolutely smooth.

Glaze coat

1 Place the oil colours on one of the plates, add the linseed oil and Japan dryers, and stir thoroughly. Finally add the white spirit (a little at a time), mixing to make a transparent, but not too liquid, glaze (like single cream).

119

MARBLING

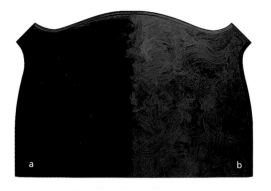

a

b

c

1

1 VERDE-NERO

a Two smooth coats of black eggshell establish the base colour.

b A crumpled, thin plastic bag pressed into the wet green glaze creates the uneven pattern.

c Small areas of semi-wet green glaze are removed with a cloth-wrapped finger to reveal parts of the black base coat.

1 The finished sample: now thread veins flow in dynamic diagonals. Thicker veins can be blurred with a dusting brush or blotted with a clean linen rag.

2 Apply an even coat to the surface, using the household paint brush. Leave to dry (12 hours).

4 Holding the scrunched up plastic bag in your hand, press it against the wet glaze to create an uneven, broken pattern over the entire surface.

5 Lightly blend the pattern with the dusting brush.

6 Using a clean rag wrapped around your index finger, remove small areas of the semi-wet glaze to reveal more of the base coat. Leave to dry (12 hours).

Adding the veins

1 Mix the oil colours on the other plate, stirring well. For a natural look, never use pure white.

2 Holding the sable brush at a 90-degree angle to the surface, draw in the veining. Always work towards yourself, twisting the brush from time to time to create the characteristically random nature of veining. Leave to dry (2–3 days).

Protective coats

Apply at least four coats of varnish, allowing 12 hours' drying between coats and sanding very lightly (and wiping clean) each time.

2 CREAM CARRARA
Follow the method for Verde-Nero. Base coat: off-white eggshell. Darker cream glaze coat: dots of zinc white, lamp black and yellow ochre, 1tsp linseed oil, 2 drops Japan dryers. Veins: dots of zinc white and payne's grey. Protection: as Verde-Nero, but be aware that varnish yellows if exposed to the sun.

2

ROSSO DI VERONA

Creating beautiful fossil-stone marbles like that shown here is surprisingly easy – it demands no painterly skills. The trick lies less in the brushwork and more in the random spatter of solvent onto the still wet glaze.

MATERIALS

Quantity for an area 2m²
Base coats ▶ 200ml pink eggshell paint (2 coats)
Glaze coat ▶ artists' oil colours: 1 dash burnt sienna, 1 dash raw sienna, 1 dash zinc white, 1 dot lamp black / ½tbsp damar resin varnish / 1tbsp white spirit
Dispersion ▶ 2tbsp white spirit
Protective coats ▶ 200ml polyurethane varnish (4 coats)

EQUIPMENT

40mm household paint brush / dustsheets / plate for mixing colour / 25mm household paint brush / saucer for dispersing spirit / mixing stick / old toothbrush / sea sponge (optional)

METHOD
Base coats

Apply a base coat to the primed, sanded and dusted surface as for Verde-Nero Marble, using pink eggshell.

Glaze coat

PROTECT YOUR WORK SPACE WITH DUSTSHEETS BEFORE YOU BEGIN. Make sure that each surface to be painted is completely flat and horizontal.

1 Place the oil colours on the plate, add the resin varnish and stir thoroughly. Then add 1 tablespoon white spirit (a little at a time), mixing to the consistency of single cream.

2 Brush the glaze on with the 40mm brush, using bold, criss-cross strokes.

3 Stipple the wet glaze with the same brush, using a gentle, tapping wrist movement to break up the brush strokes.

4 To begin dispersing the still wet glaze, dip just the tip of the 25mm brush into the saucer containing 2 tablespoons white spirit. Positioned approx. 30cm above the glazed surface, lightly tap the loaded brush against a mixing stick to flick a little white spirit over the surface. It will instantly start to 'ciss', billowing into whorls and curves.

5 Continue the process, now using the toothbrush and creating a series of smaller patterns. Leave to dry (2–3 days).

3 **ROSSO DI VERONA**
You can soften and blend the effect by waiting 1 hour after step 5 and then pressing a damp sponge onto the semi-dry surface. Leave to dry (2–3 days).

Protective coats

See Verde-Nero Marble.

WAX ON WOOD

Until the late 18th century the usual protective finish on furniture was beeswax or resin varnishes. Most furniture *cognoscenti* will agree that nothing quite equals the sheen and depth of wax applied on wood and lovingly built up and polished over the years. It not only fills the grain and pores but also enriches the colour and enhances the figuring. Although waxing is a finish that requires time and energy, wood treated in this way only improves with age, and it smells wonderful! Pure beeswax is increasingly expensive and difficult to find and the traditional method of heating the wax with the necessary turpentine solvent can be dangerous. We recommend using one of the many good proprietary waxes available – check that it is made from pure beeswax or from beeswax and carnauba wax. Avoid any wax containing silicone.

COLOURLESS WAX ON UNFINISHED WOOD

MATERIALS
Quantity for an area 2m²
100ml colourless proprietary beeswax

EQUIPMENT
2 stiff shoe brushes / superfine wirewool (grade 0000)

METHOD
1 Using one of the stiff shoe brushes (it must be scrupulously clean) and working vigorously in the direction of the grain, apply the wax to the wood. Leave to dry (1 hour).
2 Buff firmly with the other, wax-free brush, again working with the grain. Leave to dry (24 hours).
3 Repeat steps 1 and 2, making sure you use the same brush as before to put on the wax and the other to polish.
4 Apply subsequent layers of beeswax lightly with wirewool. This removes any excess wax and fills and levels the grain. The result is a flat, smooth sheen rather than a surface build-up which can become sticky and dirty.

❶ COLOURLESS
The oak glows subtly and natural figuring (seen left) is emphasized.

❷ PALE WAX
A richer effect: 1tsp raw sienna artists' oil colour has been added to the wax.

❸ DARK WAX
Just 2tsp raw umber and the grain is almost obscured: for dark pieces.

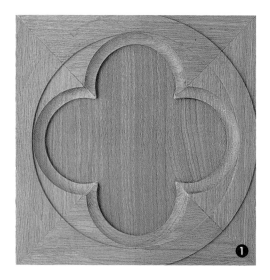

USING COLOURED WAX

The same method can be used with coloured waxes, either bought ready-made – make sure they contain beeswax – or tinted by adding very small amounts of artists' oil colour to colourless proprietary beeswax. Coloured waxes can create a richer, deeper finish. They are also useful for camouflaging new holes and joints and for unifying previously painted, stripped furniture made from different timbers, as is sometimes the case with provincial pieces.

Note There is just one principle to remember: you can wax over all finishes, including oil, paint or French polish, but you cannot apply any finish over wax.

A century of patient waxing has given this oak crib a magnificent lustre. Although new woods will require waxing once a month for a year (see step 4), for older woods, such as this crib, waxing a couple of times a year using the same method will be sufficient. For very fine pieces, use washed linen cloth instead of wirewool.

PART THREE

PROJECTS

Twelve inspirational workshop projects, described in detail from start to finish and offering a unique, over-the-shoulder account of the rationale behind the modern restorer's approach and methods when confronting a variety of simple and not-so-simple restoration problems, cross-referenced as appropriate to earlier sections of the book

Although a considerable amount of restoration work was carried out on this 19th-century, leather-topped African mahogany desk (see page 137), every effort was made to ensure that it still retained its initial character and precious, irreplaceable patina.

DINING CHAIR

Our client's five matching dining-room chairs were crying out for a sixth to complete the set. The existing chairs were made of darkly stained mahogany in the balloon-backed style popular throughout the 19th century, with turned and carved legs and seats upholstered in green velvet. Fortunately we soon found a similar chair – the back was identical, as was the stained mahogany, but the front legs had slightly different carved details. The client, however, was content: the legs would after all spend much of their life firmly under the table. The upholstery was more problematic. Not only would we have to change the faded top cover for matching velvet but the entire seating structure needed reworking – the supporting webbing had collapsed along with the layers of wadding and padding. Given the weary appearance of the chair, with its dull finish and white water mark down one leg, we could expect to find consolidation work once the upholstery was removed. Filling would also be necessary along the show wood of the rails, where stray tacks had left tiny holes.

It is an interesting exercise to date chairs not from their frames but from their upholstery, if it is still original. An early Regency-transition dining chair would have had a drop-in seat, whereas a later, post-1850s version might well have had the buoyancy of coiled springs. We estimate that this chair, with its stuff-over seat (see page 72), could date from about 1840.

JOB LIST	Remove upholstery / clean and partially strip / strengthen joints / fill tack holes / finish / re-upholster

MATERIALS	Cleaning and stripping ▶ 500ml white spirit / 250ml methylated spirits Strengthening the joints ▶150ml hot pearl glue (see page 45) Filling tack holes ▶ brown-mahogany coloured wax stick Finishing ▶ 50ml '50/50' French polish (see page 94) / 2 drops linseed oil / 100ml colourless proprietary beeswax Replacing the upholstery ▶ 3m x 5cm webbing / 1m x 130cm heavyweight hessian / upholsterers' nylon thread / 350g sifted coconut fibre / 1m x 130cm lightweight hessian / curled animal hair pad (re-used, equalled 350g / 1m x 140cm linter felt wadding / 1m x 140cm calico / 1m x 140cm cotton upholstery velvet / 2m x 15mm gimping / 30ml fabric glue

EQUIPMENT	Tack lifter / mallet / lint-free cotton rags / jug of hot water, plus heatproof bowl and saucepan, for warming glue / syringe and needle (see page 29) / sash clamps / wood offcuts for clamping / low-wattage soldering iron / wooden lollipop stick or dental tongue spline / linen cloth / 2 rubbers and storage jars (see pages 95 and 96) / superfine wirewool (grade 0000) / 2 clean shoe brushes / hand-held staple gun / webbing stretcher / scissors / tape measure / curved upholsterer's needle / regulator / double-pointed straight needle / hand protector (see page 72)

METHOD

Removing the upholstery

1 The upholstery tacks were removed with the tack lifter and mallet, working in the direction of the grain.

2 The upholstered seat was carefully dismantled and a note kept of the order in which the materials were removed.

This is an extremely important part of the process, especially when working with antique furniture. The dismantled layers of 'evidence' always provide useful guidelines for re-upholstery so throw nothing away until the job is finished. Working from the bottom up, we noted webbing, hessian, fibre stuffing, stitched hessian, a curled-hair pad, wadding, calico and, finally, four different (and decayed) top covers. Happily, this traditional, durable 'stitched, stuff-over seat' method and use of materials corresponded to that used to upholster the client's other five dining chairs. It was interesting to discover that the original 19th-century cover on our find had been black oil-cloth, treated to look like leather.

Cleaning and partial stripping

We noticed that invisible parts of the chair frame were made of beech, a common Victorian practice, and this was checked for infestation extremely carefully because beech is prone to infestation, and furniture beetles often hide under upholstery. Fortunately there was no problem.

1 The whole chair was cleaned with rags moistened with white spirit to remove the heavy build-up of old wax.

2 Because the water mark on the leg proved serious – it had cut right through the top layer of French polish – the area was stripped with methylated spirits (see page 98, Repairs).

Strengthening the joints

As suspected, the frame, without the upholstery support, needed strengthening.

1 Hot pearl glue was injected into all the joints (see page 47).

2 They were tightened with four sash clamps (see page 47) and left to dry (12 hours).

Filling tack holes

The holes dotted along the seat rails were filled, using the wax stick melted with the soldering iron (see page 87).

Finishing

1 A coat of '50/50' French polish was applied to the stripped section of the leg with the rubber (see page 98, Repairs). The process took 2 days and the leg was left to dry (1 week) before the shine was cut with wirewool (see page 97).

2 The whole chair was polished with colourless beeswax, using the shoe brushes (see page 122).

Replacing the upholstery

See page 72. Upholstery materials can sometimes be cleaned and re-cycled – in this case we could keep only the curled-hair pad but that represented a considerable saving. A small section of gimping (or trim), peeled back from one of the client's original chairs, enabled us to see the former colour of the now-faded velvet. We matched our new fabric to this, knowing that it, too, would fade and exactly match the rest in time. Basing our choice upon the faded green would have meant that within a year or two the new velvet would be much lighter than the rest. When fitting the top cover, care was taken to ensure that the velvet pile ran in the same direction as that on the other chairs.

TABLE WITH
MARBLED TOP

'Job lots' can be full of surprises. Bidding recently for a set of Louis XV reproduction chairs, we came away not just with the chairs but also this table, hideously sprayed with gold car paint and with a cut-down wardrobe door nailed on as a top. It wobbled wildly but we liked its proportions and decided to strip it, strengthen the beech-wood structure and replace the top with made-to-measure *faux* marble. However, as the hand-saw marks, the water-gilded rim and the finesse of the decoration were slowly revealed, we realized that we had found not a modern copy but a genuine antique. This was truly satisfying restoration work since the expected transformation was accompanied by a wonderful sense of discovery. Sadly, the chairs revealed only a bad case of (treatable) 20th-century woodworm.

JOB LIST	Remove plywood top / strip paint / remove gesso / strengthen / apply new gesso / repaint base / wax / replace top / marble top / varnish top

MATERIALS

Stripping the paint ▶ 1 litre solvent-based stripper / 50ml white spirit
Removing the gesso ▶ 1 bucket hot water
Strengthening the joints ▶ 50ml hot pearl glue (see page 45)
Applying gesso (see page 100) ▶ 170ml rabbit-skin glue size / 1 litre gesso
Aged paint finish on the base ▶ 125ml glue tempera paint (see page 108): 50ml gesso, 50ml rabbit-skin glue size, 25ml water, artists' gouache colours – 2 dashes zinc white, 1 dash raw umber, 1 dash yellow ochre, 1 dash lamp black (2 coats), plus 1 dash black and ochre for first coat
Waxing ▶ 100ml colourless proprietary beeswax / 2–3tsp raw umber artists' powder pigment / 1tsp rottenstone / 1tsp white spirit
Replacing the top ▶ 18mm pine boards / 100ml hot pearl glue
Marbling the top ▶ 40ml rabbit-skin glue size / 250ml gesso for 2 primer coats / 100ml light grey eggshell paint for 2 base coats / glaze coat: artists' oil colours – 1 dash lamp black, 1 dash zinc white, 1 dot raw umber, plus ½tbsp linseed oil, 1 drop Japan dryers, 1tbsp white spirit / veining: artists' oil colours – 1 dash titanium white, 1 small dot lamp black
Varnishing the top ▶ 100ml colourless satin polyurethane varnish (4 coats)

EQUIPMENT

Rubber hammer / pliers / industrial gloves / 25mm household paint brush / flexible plastic filling knife / craft knife / blunted paint knife / coarse wirewool (grade 2) / lint-free cotton rags / medium wirewool (grade 0) / 2 heatproof bowls and saucepan for warming glue and size / syringe and needle (see page 29) / webbing clamp / gesso brush / linen rag to smooth gesso / mask / stiff shoe brush / duster / hairdryer / small glue brush / sash clamps / wood offcuts for clamping / jack plane / jigsaw / 80-grade sandpaper / 40mm household paint brush / 240-grade sandpaper / 2 plates / thin plastic bag / dusting brush / round sable brush / 40mm varnish brush

TABLE WITH MARBLED TOP

METHOD
Removing the top

The plywood top was roughly held in position by panel pins; some were gently tapped out from beneath with a rubber hammer, the remainder were removed with pliers. Its only merit was a good fit so it was reserved for use as a template.

Stripping
the paint

A test strip was unnecessary. Close inspection showed that the gleaming gold car paint had been applied to mask a decayed paint surface which had obviously deteriorated too far to make the frankly difficult task of removing the synthetic 'gilding' worthwhile. Prising off a loose chip revealed a gesso base – an early indication that the table was perhaps older than we thought.

1 Solvent-based stripper was applied to the whole surface with the household paint brush (see page 40) and we were surprised to find water gilding (see page 103) all round the top rim. Although it is not harmed by solvent-based strippers, it was important to proceed with great caution.

2 The flexible plastic filling knife was trimmed with the craft knife to mirror the profile of the curved rim and then used to remove the sticky paint and stripper mix without disturbing the gilding.

3 On the remaining surfaces, including the moulding, we used the blunted paint knife and wirewool to remove any traces of stripper and then neutralized with white spirit.

Removing the
gesso

Once all the paint was off, we could see that the gesso (see page 100) was unstable and crumbled to the touch. It was all removed, using a bucket of hot water and medium-grade wirewool, and the piece was then dried with rags and left for 12 hours. Careful, gentle rubbing was essential if we were not to damage the wood or – as we could now clearly see – the delicate *rocaille* hand carving.

Strengthening the
joints

Although the legs were solidly attached, the central x-frame stretcher was loose, which meant that the table was very unsteady. To avoid dismantling, and possibly damaging, the piece, we decided to stabilize the joints in this area.

1 Hot pearl glue was injected into the joints (see page 47) between the stretcher and the legs.

2 The joints were then secured with a webbing clamp (see page 28) and left to dry (12 hours).

Applying gesso

Size was applied to all visible surfaces except the gilded rim, using the gesso brush (see page 101), followed by six even coats of gesso, which was left to dry (6 days) and wet polished (see page 101).

Aged paint finish on the base

See page 108 for the preparation of glue tempera paint and the technique used on the gessoed surfaces. In this instance, two coats of slightly different tone were mixed – the first *darker* than the second – using zinc white, raw umber, yellow ochre and lamp black as colourants. The full quantity was prepared, divided between two containers, and dashes of lamp black and yellow ochre were added to the first coat. Once the table had been distressed for the 'antique' finish, it was left to dry fully (24 hours).

Waxing

ALWAYS WEAR A MASK WHEN USING POWDER PIGMENTS.

1 Using 95ml beeswax as a base (see page 110), antiquing wax was applied to all surfaces except the gilded rim, both to protect and to cut the new look of the paint finish.

2 The remaining beeswax was rubbed gently into the gilding with clean rags to protect against water damage and buffed.

Replacing the top

The original table top would have been marble but for reasons of cost and weight we opted for a top made from four pine boards, bought from a professional timber yard to ensure uniformly seasoned wood (see page 14).

1 Hot pearl glue was brushed onto the adjoining surfaces (see page 46) and the boards were sash clamped (see page 47) and left to dry (12 hours).

2 The glued boards were clamped to a sturdy work surface and the facing side was planed to ensure a flat top.

3 Using the plywood as a template, the outline was traced onto the surface and the new top cut out with a jigsaw.

4 Its top and edges were smoothed with 80-grade sandpaper and it was checked for fit.

Marbling the top

See page 119 (Verde-Nero Marble) for the technique – we decided, however, to imitate the white-veined grey marble we had seen on a similar piece. First the surface was sized and then primed with two even coats of gesso, allowing 1–2 hours for each coat to dry, and wet polished as before.

Varnishing the top

See page 120. Four coats of varnish were applied to the marbled surface. Two would have protected the top, but many more coats (up to a dozen) could have been added for the smooth polished look of real marble – four was a reasonable compromise.

LEATHER-TOPPED
DESK

A family 'hand-me-down', this double-fronted desk had been stored in a damp basement for several years and was in need of care and restoration. Made from African mahogany, with brass drawer handles and a fine burgundy-coloured leather top, it had aspirations to the Regency style but was in fact a mid-19th century design popular in Britain and the United States. Although it had an attractive patina, much of the wood had dulled and was badly water-marked. A corner moulding had been knocked off on one side and about 1910 a great-uncle, in typical schoolboy fashion, had carved his initials on the desk rim. The leather top was scuffed and scratched and the drawers had swollen and jammed due to the damp storage. Once revitalized, the desk was all set for another century of service. Great uncle's initials, although now less visible, were not removed – they were, after all, part of the desk's 'narrative' and sensitive restoration should always take this into account.

JOB LIST

Remove drawers / protect legs and leather top / strip rest of wooden carcase / replace corner moulding / sand / (possible) stain / French polish / wax / renovate leather

LEATHER - TOPPED DESK

MATERIALS

Stripping ▶ 1 litre solvent-based paint stripper / 50ml white spirit
Replacing the corner moulding ▶ 6 x 70mm plywood offcut / 8 x 60mm
African mahogany offcut / 2tbsp hot pearl glue (see page 45)
French polishing (see page 94) ▶ 200ml 'pure' polish / 200ml '50/50' polish /
2tsp linseed oil / 100ml methylated spirits
Staining ▶ 1tsp medium mahogany nitro stain
Waxing ▶ 50ml colourless proprietary beeswax
Renovating the leather ▶ 2tbsp red mahogany nitro stain / 50ml neutral
leather cream

EQUIPMENT

Newspaper / low-tack masking tape / scissors / industrial gloves /
25mm household paint brush / blunted paint knife / medium wirewool
(grade 0) / lint-free cotton rags / steel rule / fretsaw / paring chisel /
hairdryer / heatproof bowl and saucepan for warming glue / small glue
brush / deep-throat G-clamp / wood offcut / 80-grade sandpaper /
120-grade sandpaper / 2 rubbers and storage jars (see pages 95 and 96) /
180-grade silicone-carbide paper / spirit-resistant vinyl gloves / round
sable brush / candle / superfine wirewool (grade 0000) / duster

METHOD
Removing drawers

Both drawers were carefully tugged free of the carcase and
placed in a warm place for 'shrinkage' (see page 37).

Protecting the patina

The legs, like the drawer fronts, had acquired a desirable,
hard-to-fake patina which we wanted to preserve, and the
leather top had to be covered before work began on the
carcase. Both were protected with newspaper secured with
masking tape. (Always use low-tack tape near delicate
surfaces – sticky tape can remove paint, patina or leather.)

Stripping

See page 39. Water had penetrated right through the
original French polish and into the wood, obliging us to strip
and neutralize all visible surfaces.

Replacing the corner moulding

1 The inexpensive plywood offcut was measured, cut and
trimmed, using the fretsaw and paring chisel, to establish the
profile of the missing piece.
2 Once a good fit had been achieved, the mahogany offcut
was cut to shape, using the plywood piece as a template.
3 Hot pearl glue (see page 46) was brushed onto both
surfaces and the mahogany piece was carefully positioned.
The surrounding surfaces were wiped immediately to ensure
no glue remained to interfere with later staining.
4 The piece was secured with the deep-throat G-clamp (see
page 47) and left to dry (12 hours).
5 It was then shaped to the exact profile of the surrounding
moulding, using the chisel and 80-grade sandpaper.

Sanding

All visible parts of the carcase were then lightly rubbed with 120-grade sandpaper, using a circular motion, and dusted with damp cotton rags.

Finishing

1 See page 94 for French polishing. As expected, once the first coat of polish had been applied to the visible surfaces with the rubber, it was clear that the colour of the new moulding was slightly lighter.

2 The new piece was stained with medium mahogany (see page 114, but using a sable brush), and left to dry (4 hours). The initial coat of polish had ensured that the stain would not leach into the surrounding wood.

3 French polishing was resumed and, when the process was complete (4 days, plus a week's drying time), the newspaper protection on the legs and leather top was removed.

4 The drawer runners were rubbed with candle wax to ensure a smooth glide and the drawers, now back to their original size, slid easily into place.

5 A protective coat of colourless beeswax was applied to the new French polish with superfine wirewool (see page 97, Cutting the Shine) to create a flat sheen that matched the patina on the legs and drawers.

6 The worst scratches on the leather top were touched up, using the red mahogany stain (as above), again applied with the sable brush and left to dry (4 hours). A light touch was essential here: heavily restored leather is rarely convincing and, again, we wanted the piece to tell its story.

7 Leather cream was applied, and then buffed with a duster.

REGENCY
SABRE-LEG CHAIR

This elegant Regency chair, inspired by the designs of Thomas Hope, the Scottish-born style arbiter of the early 19th century, was a generous gift from friends redecorating and with no use for a single chair. (Do remember when buying old furniture that single chairs are harder to sell – and thus comparatively cheaper – than those sold in pairs or sets. You can easily build up an inexpensive, adaptable 'singles' collection ranging from Chippendale to Chinese export, which comes in useful when furnishing small spaces.) The chair was made of beech, typical of painted furniture of this period; it was structurally sound and the caning had been professionally replaced. The problem lay in the recent, careless application of black household enamel paint intended to 'restore' areas of worn paintwork, such as the chair back and arm rests: the result was an uneven, messy surface and a synthetic tone in conflict with the original dark hue. In addition, the gold coach-lining and foliage motifs, both integral parts of the chair's decoration, were partially obscured by a layer of discoloured shellac varnish. It was clear that restoration would need a delicate hand and infinite patience.

JOB LIST

Test strip / remove modern enamel paint, wax and old shellac / apply gesso / repaint stripped surfaces / retouch coach-lines and painted motifs / varnish with shellac polish / wax

MATERIALS

Test strip ▶ 1tsp white spirit / 1tsp methylated spirits
Removing the varnish ▶ 500ml methylated spirits
Applying gesso (see page 100) ▶ 50ml rabbit-skin glue size / 100ml gesso
Restoring the paintwork ▶ artists' gouache colours: 2 dashes ivory black, 1 dash raw umber, 1 dot zinc white / 1tsp water
Coach-lining ▶ artists' gouache colours: 2 dashes bronze, 1 dash raw sienna / ¼tsp water
Varnishing with shellac ▶ 100ml transparent shellac polish (see page 33)
Waxing ▶ 25ml colourless proprietary beeswax

EQUIPMENT

Cotton buds / spirit-resistant vinyl gloves / cottonwool / heatproof bowl and saucepan for warming size / gesso brush / linen rag for smoothing gesso / 2 plates / clean 15mm varnish brush / no. 3 sable liner brush / rubber and storage jars (see pages 95 and 96) / lint-free cotton rag / duster

METHOD

Test strip

See page 38. White spirit was gently applied to a small patch of the original paintwork on the back chair rail – a suitably inconspicuous place – and the resulting brown mark on the cotton bud indicated a layer of wax. Rubbing the same small patch with methylated spirits again produced a brown mark on the cotton bud, indicating that the chair had also been given a protective coat of shellac.

If the black had come off, we would have stopped immediately. It would have been a signal that the original paint was being removed. However, alcohol, in *small* doses, should not remove oil paint, which, given the date of the chair, was the most likely paint to have been used.

Removing the varnish

With great care, using cottonwool pads just moistened with methylated spirits, the chair surface was gently rubbed. This gradually dissolved the discoloured shellac and enamel paint applied over it. Where even more caution was needed – over decoration – cotton buds were used instead. Slowly the painted details emerged more clearly and when no more discoloration was visible on the pads or buds, it was clear all the wax, shellac and enamel paint had been removed.

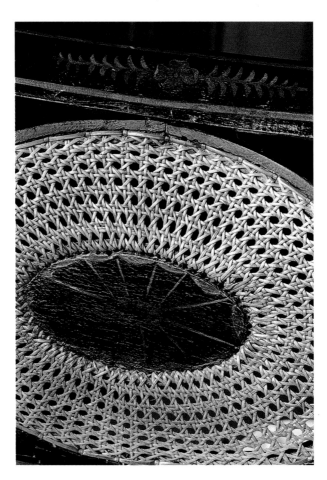

Applying gesso

The original black paint had come up very well and the places where the enamel paint had been were now bare wood. Size was applied to the bare patches, using the gesso brush, and then two layers of fine gesso were mixed and brushed on, left to dry (6 days) and wet polished (see page 101). This created an even surface on which to apply the black gouache paint and raised the bare areas to the level of the original paintwork.

Restoring the paintwork

We chose to use gouache because it covers well and has an antique quality and colour tone, when mixed with touches of zinc white and raw umber, that would blend nicely with the existing paintwork. It can also be removed, if necessary, without damaging surrounding paint.

1 The ivory black gouache was squeezed onto one of the plates, mixed with tiny amounts of raw umber and zinc white, and thinned to the consistency of single cream with water (added a little at a time, stirring constantly).

2 The paint was applied in the direction of the grain, using the varnish brush, and left to dry thoroughly (24 hours).

Coach-lining

1 The bronze gouache paint was mixed on the other plate with a minute quantity of burnt sienna to cut the glare of the new 'gold' and thinned with water as above.

2 To achieve those crisp coach-lines a steady hand is needed so it is wise to practise on an offcut first. The sable liner brush was held between thumb and forefinger while the third finger rested on the edge of the chair as a guide. The lines were left to dry (12 hours). Fortunately the painted foliage needed no retouching.

Varnishing with shellac

A shellac protection was applied to the painted surfaces, using the rubber (see page 98, Shellac Polish as Varnish), and left to dry (3 days).

Waxing

For extra protection while retaining much of the shine, colourless proprietary beeswax was rubbed on with lint-free rags and later buffed with the duster. All the chair needed now was a smart, striped cushion.

PAINTED
WASHSTAND

We found this painted pine piece in a small auction in Nice. It was part of a job lot of miscellaneous painted items and was so badly chipped and broken that we hesitated to give it workroom space. The circular top was cracked and warped, two of its three legs were precariously loose, struts and moulded details were missing or damaged. We could see, nevertheless, despite the layers of yellowed varnish and grime, that it had considerable charm with its painted and decorated surface of faded greens, dusty blues and even the odd glint of gold.

It is always a plus to find pieces with original paintwork still intact. However damaged this may be, resist the temptation to strip and start anew. There is a beauty in old, barely-there colours that is hard to replicate: in this case even the yellow varnish contributed to the mellow effect. We also knew that, once the piece was repaired and restored, we could give a contemporary function to this 1900s washstand: with a simple, large ceramic bowl and a handsome green fern inserted into the circular top it would make a perfect plant stand.

JOB LIST
Clean / repair top /
strengthen carcase /
secure and level legs /
replace missing and
damaged struts and
mouldings / patch gesso /
restore paint / restore
gilding / varnish /
patinate with wax

PAINTED WASHSTAND

MATERIALS

Cleaning ▶ concentrated technical soap (see page 38) and warm water
Repairing the top and carcase ▶ 3 x 30mm pine slivers / 60ml hot pearl glue (see page 45)
Repairing legs, struts and shelf ▶ 6 wood screws / 16 x 20mm pine struts / 60ml hot pearl glue / small pieces of pine offcut for shelf moulding / 16 x 20mm pine offcut for turned foot
Surface restoration ▶ 50ml rabbit-skin glue size (see page 100) / 1 litre gesso (see page 100) / artists' gouache colours: 1 dash azure blue, dots of lamp black, burnt sienna, carmine red, chrome green light, Prussian blue, raw sienna, raw umber, ultramarine blue, zinc white / 25g red bole / 2tbsp methylated spirits / 6 sheets 23.75-carat gold leaf / 2tbsp water
Finishing ▶ 125ml artists' clear matt picture varnish / ½tsp yellow ochre artists' powder pigment / 100ml colourless proprietary beeswax / artists' powder pigments: ½tsp ivory black, 1 tsp raw umber

EQUIPMENT

Sponge / circular saw / steel rule / crosscut saw / hairdryer / 2 heatproof bowls and saucepan for warming glue, size and wax / small glue brush / webbing clamp / small plane / paring chisel / mallet / rasp / syringe and needle (see page 29) / screwdriver / 4 wedges (see page 49) / spirit level / adhesive mastic / block plane / gent's saw / sash clamp / G-clamp / wood offcut / gesso brush / linen rag / round sable brushes / lint-free rags / dusting brush / camel mop / aluminium-oxide paper / soft bristle brush / cottonwool / gilder's knife / gilder's cushion / squirrel mop / gilder's tip / agate burnisher / 240-grade sandpaper / mask / small container / saucer

METHOD
Cleaning

See page 38. The painted surfaces were carefully sponged down with a gentle solution of technical soap.

Repairing the top and carcase

The cracked and warped circular top had been glued and nailed onto the carcase, which was constructed from curved pieces of wood staggered like the bricks in a wall and glued, making it impossible to dismantle without destroying the surviving paintwork. The solution was to enlarge the four cracks and plug, using gesso to disguise the warping.

1 Adjusting the depth of cut on the circular saw to 26mm (to match the depth of the top), the cracks were very carefully increased in depth and width to take slivers of pine.

2 The resulting cracks were measured and four pine slivers cut to size, using the circular saw and small crosscut saw.

3 Each sliver was brushed with hot pearl glue (see page 46), positioned and clamped securely using the webbing clamp (see page 47). When the glue was dry (12 hours), the slivers were planed and then shaped with the chisel and rasp.

4 Hot pearl glue was injected into all cracks on the carcase (see page 47). This was securely bound with the webbing clamp and then left to dry (12 hours).

Repairing legs, struts and shelf

1 The legs were screwed to the interior carcase and levelled (see page 49).

2 The two replacement struts were cut to replace the missing struts – making tenon joints for the mortises in the legs and half joints for the shelf (see page 43). The struts were then fitted, glued, left to dry (12 hours) and planed.

3 Small pieces of pine offcut were used to restore the circular rim of the shelf, which had broken off in places. These were glued, left to dry (12 hours) and then shaped with the chisel and rasp.

4 Half of one foot was also missing and this was replaced in the same way, using the larger pine offcut, secured with the G-clamp and trimmed to match with a chisel and rasp when dry.

Surface restoration

Delicate floral sprays in carmine, ochre and azure had been painted on a blue-grey ground which layers of protective varnish had yellowed, and the water gilding on the circular top and lower shelf had deteriorated considerably.

1 See page 100. Size and gesso were applied to all the bare surfaces to build them to the level of the original paintwork; they were then left to dry (6 days) and wet polished.

2 Using artists' gouache paints, recommended for their opacity and traditional colours, the missing paintwork was touched in with sable brushes. Only one coat was needed.

3 Red bole was applied over the gesso masking areas of missing gilding (see page 103), and the water gilding was replaced (see page 104). Yellow bole was omitted as we were repairing such small sections (in the spirit of the original, less than fastidious Italian gilder). Once complete, the gilding was rubbed gently with 240-grade sandpaper until the distressed surface resembled the original gilding.

Finishing

ALWAYS WEAR A MASK WHEN USING POWDER PIGMENTS.

1 The matt picture varnish was mixed with the yellow ochre powder pigment in the small container and brushed thinly onto the newly applied paint with the camel mop, blending it carefully into the existing varnish.

2 Colourless beeswax polish was mixed with the ivory black and raw umber powder pigments (see page 110, but gently applied with rags rather than a shoe brush) to create a patina homogenizing the new paint and the old.

EMPIRE-STYLE
NIGHT TABLE

We were both amused to discover the stamp of the great French cabinet-maker Jacob-Desmalter (1770–1841) on this Empire-style auction find. A Jacob piece it certainly was not: its thin veneer of African mahogany laid on a pine carcase, mass-produced brass fittings, contradictory constructional and stylistic details all betrayed its early 20th-century fabrication. Unusual dimensions and a compartment with a sliding (tambour) door indicated its initial use as a chamber-pot cupboard. Once restored, it could, we felt, make a stylish telephone table. Although well made, the piece needed considerable attention. A carelessly placed hot object had blistered the top, the brass mounts were discoloured, inappropriate handles had replaced missing fittings and the door was jammed open. Unloved and unpolished, it looked completely lifeless.

JOB LIST

Remove brass fittings / dismantle tambour door / strip shellac / repair door / replace veneer top / restore brass fittings / stain new veneer / French polish / wax / 'antique' new handles / refit

MATERIALS

Stripping ▶ 2 litres solvent-based paint stripper / 150ml white spirit
Repairing the door ▶ fine canvas or linen, dark colour and pre-washed (52 x 21cm) / 60ml hot pearl glue (see page 45) / French polishing (see page 94): 50ml 'pure' polish, 50ml '50/50' polish, 1tsp linseed oil, 25ml methylated spirits
Replacing the veneer ▶ 1.2mm African mahogany veneer (50 x 60cm) / 60ml hot pearl glue
Restoring the brass fittings ▶ 2–3tbsp solvent-based paint stripper / 1tbsp white spirit / 50ml colourless metal lacquer
Finishing ▶ 1tbsp white spirit / 50ml light red mahogany nitro stain / French polishing: 100ml 'pure' polish, 100ml '50/50' polish, 2tsp linseed oil, 50ml methylated spirits / 50ml colourless proprietary beeswax / 2 small brass knobs / 1tbsp cold patination fluid / 15ml micro-crystalline wax

EQUIPMENT

Screwdriver / card to 'file' screws / syringe and needle (see page 29) / industrial gloves / 25mm household paint brush / blunted paint knife / medium wirewool (grade 0) / lint-free cotton rags / 18mm chipboard / 6 x 15mm ramin battening / steel rule / tenon saw / 12 panel pins / hammer / scissors / hairdryer / heatproof bowl and saucepan for warming glue / small and large glue brushes / 2 rubbers and storage jars (see pages 95 and 96) / 180-grade silicone-carbide paper / superfine wirewool (grade 0000) / small G-clamps / wood offcuts/ large cotton cloth / iron / household sponge / veneer hammer / craft knife / newspaper / chipboard to protect top / sash clamps / camel mop / 120-grade sandpaper / spirit-resistant vinyl gloves / fine wirewool (grade 000)

EMPIRE - STYLE NIGHT TABLE

METHOD
Dismantling

The tambour door was jammed because the fabric backing, which also formed the 'hinge', had completely disintegrated. Fortunately we were able to remove the door from the carcase – a jammed door complicates repairs considerably.

1 All the brass fittings were unscrewed and the screws were pushed through numbered cards for later return to their original positions.

2 Using the syringe filled with hot water, the joint of the batten holding the tambour door in place was injected to dissolve the glue.

3 Once the batten was loose, it was possible to slide it out, followed by the remaining slats, which were numbered in their order of removal.

Stripping

We could see that the piece had been French polished so a strip test was unnecessary, but someone less experienced would have found that a cotton bud dipped in methylated spirits removed the brown shellac finish. The entire surface, including the tambour door, was carefully stripped and neutralized (see page 39), leaving the patina undisturbed so that the piece would retain its 'antique' look.

Repairing the door

1 Using the chipboard as a base and two pairs of parallel battens for the sides, a tray was constructed to contain the numbered slats precisely and tightly when placed façade side down in their original sequence. Three of the battens were initially pinned in place, leaving one end batten free until the slats had been positioned.

2 A rag wrung out in hot water softened the old glue which held the perished backing fabric in position, and it was then removed with the blunted paint knife.

3 The canvas, once measured and cut to size, was glued into position to replace the backing (see page 46) and left to dry (12 hours).

4 The door was French polished (the whole process took 4 days, see page 94) and it was then left to dry (1 week).

5 It was remounted in its track and the securing door batten was reglued (as above), held fast with G-clamps (see page 47), and left to dry (12 hours).

Replacing the veneer

Once the piece had been stripped, we could see that the mahogany veneer on the top was too badly damaged to restore. Matching it was simple because African mahogany is still available (see page 18). For Removing Old Veneer, see page 93; for replacing veneer, see page 89. Note: unusually we clamped the hammered veneer – it was particularly thick.

Restoring the brass fittings

The brass mounts, typical of the Empire style, had been covered in a shellac-based ormolu varnish, which had dulled and discoloured. For cleaning metal fittings, see page 69 (introduction to Antiquing Metal Fittings). After thorough drying, a thin layer of colourless metal lacquer was brushed on and the fittings were left to dry in a warm place (8 hours).

Finishing

1 The new veneer top was stained to match the old (see page 114, Using Nitro Stains) and left to dry (6 hours).

2 The whole piece was finely sanded, using 120-grade sandpaper, and dusted with damp lint-free rags.

3 The surface was then French polished (again, the process took 4 days, see page 94) and it was left to dry (1 week).

4 A final protective coat of beeswax was applied with wirewool (see page 97, Cutting the Shine).

5 The brass mounts were refitted, using the original numbered screws, and the inappropriate drop handles were replaced by simple brass knobs found in a local hardware store and 'antiqued' (see page 69).

CHEST OF
DRAWERS

This late 18th-century chest of drawers, eminently practical and just the right size for today's small apartments, had been in constant use for years – probably ever since it was first made. Small wonder then that all the drawer runners were worn out, making drawer movement difficult and jerky. This poor alignment had torn patches of veneer off the carcase around the drawer fronts, and some stringing (the flat inlay that edged the drawers) was also missing. One of the feet had cracked off and, although the brass drawer handles were original (often not the case due to the Victorian mania for replacing brass handles with wooden knobs), one of the back plates was missing. The mahogany veneer, laid on a pine carcase, had aged well – the colour and patina were most attractive – but the top of the chest was damaged by stains and scratches.

JOB LIST

Clean and strip / repair drawer runners and sides / re-glue foot / replace missing veneer and stringing / French polish new top, veneer and stringing / model and 'antique' back plate

CHEST OF DRAWERS

MATERIALS

Cleaning and stripping ▶ 1 litre white spirit / 500ml solvent-based paint stripper / 1tbsp white spirit / 500ml methylated spirits
Repairing the runners and sides ▶ 20 x 20mm pine fillets / 150ml hot pearl glue (see page 45) / 12 flat-headed nails / 8 x 18mm pine slivers
Regluing the foot ▶ 50ml hot pearl glue
Replacing veneer ▶ 3mm Honduras mahogany pieces / 50ml hot pearl glue
Replacing stringing ▶ 3 x 3mm Indian rosewood strip / 50ml hot pearl glue
French polishing (see page 94) ▶ 100ml 'pure' polish / 100ml '50/50' polish / 2tsp linseed oil / 50ml methylated spirits
Moulding and antiquing the back plate ▶ 150ml silicone moulding rubber and catalyst to suit / 50ml polyester resin and catalyst to suit / 2tbsp brass filler / metal polish / brown cold-patination fluid (see page 69) / 1tsp micro-crystalline wax

EQUIPMENT

Spirit-resistant vinyl gloves / lint-free cotton rags / industrial gloves / 25mm household paint brush / blunted paint knife / medium wirewool (grade 0) / mortise chisel / locking tape measure / tenon saw / hairdryer / heatproof bowl and saucepan for warming glue / small glue brush / hammer / speed clamps / sash clamps / wood offcuts for clamping / paring chisel / low-angled block plane / large batten for clamping sides / household sponge / gent's saw / greaseproof paper / plywood block for clamping / low-tack masking tape / 180-grade sandpaper / 2 rubbers and storage jars (see pages 95 and 96) / 180-grade silicone-carbide paper / plasticine / sheet A4 paper / 2 flexible plastic containers / hacksaw / 120-grade sandpaper / superfine wirewool (grade 0000) / soft cloth / cottonwool / fine wirewool (grade 000) / electric drill and 5mm metal bit

METHOD
Cleaning and stripping

1 The whole piece was wiped with white spirit (see page 38).
2 The badly damaged top surface was stripped and then neutralized with white spirit (see page 39). We took care not to strip the sides. As with many modest pieces of this date, they were not veneered but painted *faux bois*.
3 A layer of old shellac was also stripped off the façade, using methylated spirits (see page 98, Repairs).

Repairing the runners and sides

All the pine runners were replaced (see page 65): six in all as bottom drawers do not need them and the central runner for the top drawers was oak and still in good shape. All 10 drawer sides were built up with pine slivers (see page 66).

Regluing the foot

Closer examination showed that the foot had cracked along the original glue line, making a clean break which required little veneer repair. (For those less fortunate, see page 62.)
1 Once the chest had been laid on its back on the floor, the surfaces that were to be stuck together were sponged with hot water, dried with a rag, and left for 1 hour.

2 Both surfaces were brushed with hot pearl glue (see page 46), secured with two sash clamps (see page 47), and left to dry (12 hours).

Replacing the veneer

See page 91, Patching Veneer. Speed clamps were secured and left on for 12 hours. In awkward areas masking tape was used instead of clamps. We store every scrap of veneer left from previous jobs in transparent plastic wallets and usually manage to find a near-match for small repairs. Veneer suppliers can also be generous with their throw-outs. The small pieces of Honduras mahogany used were levelled with the low-angled block plane.

Replacing the stringing

The original stringing was stained fruitwood: we found a match in Indian rosewood and so avoided tricky staining.

1 The sections of rosewood were measured and cut to size with the gent's saw.

2 The rebates were wiped clean, using a rag and hot water.

3 Hot pearl glue was brushed into the rebates and onto the pieces of stringing, which were then bedded in position. When the glue was partially set – that is, had a stiff jelly-like consistency – the surrounding surfaces were cleaned again.

4 All the sections of stringing were 'clamped' with masking tape and left to dry (12 hours).

French polishing

1 The stripped top surface was rubbed down lightly with 180-grade sandpaper, dusted with a damp rag, then French polished (the whole process took 4 days, see page 94) and left to dry (1 week).

2 A coat of 50/50 polish was also applied to the new stringing and veneer inserts, using the appropriate rubbers to blend the old shellac with the new (see page 98, Repairs).

Modelling and antiquing the back plate

Although hardware stores and mail-order firms offer a wide choice of reproduction fittings, the perfect match is often elusive. In this case we had to make our own.

WEAR MASK AND GLOVES WHEN ANTIQUING.

1 See pages 67 and 69 for making a new back plate and antiquing the surface.

2 Holes were drilled on the new backplate to correspond with those on the drawer fronts, using the electric drill fitted with the 5mm bit, and the plate was positioned and then secured by tightening the nuts on the handle bearings inside the drawer.

GILDED MIRROR

Commercial gold or bronze paint slapped on to camouflage damaged gilding is a recurring problem for restorers. It is no coincidence that much of this paint was applied post 1920, when central heating began to be more widely used and the ensuing fluctuations of temperature and humidity destroyed many gilded surfaces or their gesso support. This beautiful convex mirror and carved wood frame, c. 1810, with an ebonized eagle cresting and ball-decorated moulding, typical of a design enduringly fashionable in both Britain and North America, had been coated with treacly bronze paint. Loose candle brackets, missing decoration and an alarmingly volatile eagle's wing further contributed to its lacklustre appearance. Given the date and design of the piece, it was likely that the mirror was originally water gilded. We were aware that if we decided to strip we might find very little gilding intact and could be faced with weeks of patient surface repair before re-gilding.

JOB LIST

Test strip / clean / dismantle / strip / small repairs / apply gesso / gild / re-assemble / patinate

MATERIALS

Test strip ▶ 1tsp white spirit / 1tsp methylated spirits / 1tsp solvent-based paint stripper
Cleaning ▶ 2tsp white spirit
Stripping ▶ 500ml special-formula proprietary stripper (see page 156) / 75ml white spirit
Repairs ▶ 3 small wooden balls / 3 panel pins / 2tbsp hot pearl glue (see page 45) / 12 x 20mm limewood fillet / 1m twine / 1tbsp brass polish / 1tbsp transparent shellac polish (see page 33)
Applying the gesso (see page 100) ▶ 80ml rabbit-skin glue size / 500ml gesso
Gilding ▶ 50ml rabbit-skin glue size / 15g pale ochre bole / 15g grey bole / ½tbsp methylated spirits / gilding water (see page 104, Applying the leaf, step 1): 1tbsp rabbit-skin glue size, 400ml water, 100ml clear alcohol / 75 leaves 23.5 carat loose gold leaf (25 in a book)
Re-assembly ▶ 2tbsp methylated spirits / 2 non-drip candles / 3mm eyelet / 1 gold-plated chain
Patination ▶ 1tbsp rabbit-skin glue size / 50ml water / 1tbsp rottenstone

EQUIPMENT

Cotton buds / cottonwool / screwdriver / old blanket / pliers / cardboard to 'file' balls / 15mm house painting brush / electric drill / pin hammer / 60-grade sandpaper / household sponge / blunted paint knife / 2 heatproof bowls and saucepan for warming glue and size / small glue brush / small firmer gouge / lint-free cotton rags / camel mop / gesso brush / wood offcuts for clamping / linen rag for smoothing gesso / dental scraper / dusting brush / 500-grade aluminium oxide paper / soft bristle brush / gilder's knife / gilder's cushion / squirrel mop / 2 gilder's tips / agate burnisher / cardboard to mask mirror / chamois leather

GILDED MIRROR

METHOD

Test strip

Only dirt showed up on the cotton buds when we applied first white spirit and then methylated spirits (see page 38) so we tested with a solvent-based paint stripper, which removed the paint and revealed the gilding beneath. This was clearly water gilding – oil gilding would have been removed by the stripper.

Cleaning

Dismantling would be necessary for thorough stripping and for making individual repairs so at this stage we simply cleaned the frame, using cottonwool and white spirit. The dust was collected and set aside for final patination.

Dismantling

1 The mirror and its inner slip frame were unscrewed from the principal frame, wrapped in a blanket and stored.

2 The carved eagle, candle supports and lower foliate decoration were detached, using pliers.

3 The decorative balls attached to the frame with metal pins (42 in all, three missing) were turned to loosen and mounted in order on a card. This order was maintained throughout restoration so that they could be mounted as before.

Stripping

This was clearly going to be a delicate, time-consuming task, given the fragility of the gilded surface and the intricacy of the carving. A gilding specialist recommended a proprietary stripper containing dichloromethane and methanol.

1 The stripper was carefully applied in small (10cm) sections, using a 15mm house painting brush.

2 It was removed using cottonwool moistened with white spirit and taking care to avoid abrasions. The stripper instructions had indicated methylated spirits but we feared the water content in meths. Only one coat was necessary.

The soft brilliance of the revealed gilding was marred by blank patches of damaged gesso and even bare wood. At least a third of the frame was affected. We now had a major decision to make. Should we painstakingly re-gesso and re-gild the damaged areas using over 70 sheets of expensive gold leaf? (Patching up always involves wastage.) Or should we completely strip the piece and start from zero? (This considerably easier job would not require substantially more gold leaf.) Despite the extra work involved, we decided to retain the original gilding. It had survived almost 200 years, the patina was gorgeous and the eventual value of the piece would amply justify the time spent on it.

Small repairs

1 The three new wooden balls (bought in a craft shop) were mounted on pins, profiled to size using the electric drill chuck, and sanded roughly, ready for gesso.

2 The eagle's broken wing was thoroughly cleaned of old glue (see page 38). The adjoining faces were then brushed with hot pearl glue (see page 45), 'nudged' in, and then left to dry (12 hours).

3 The missing wooden tassel on the candelabra was re-carved from a fillet of limewood, using the small firmer gouge. As wood will not stick directly onto metal, twine was wrapped around the metal support to provide a secure surface, and the tassel was glued into position as above.

4 The brass candle holders were re-polished and sealed with shellac (see page 98, Shellac Polish as Varnish).

Applying the gesso and gilding

All damaged surfaces – including the 45 balls – were sized (see page 101) and re-gessoed (see page 102, Patching with Gesso), then re-gilded (see page 103, Water Gilding). This represented three weeks of intermittent but highly focused work – definitely not for the faint-hearted! In order to match the original gilding exactly, we took a small section of the frame to a gilding supplier. From the 12 shades of gold leaf in stock we chose a rich amber tone. The boles were also matched to the original period colours: pale ochre and grey.

Re-assembly

1 The piece was carefully re-assembled by hand. No hammer was needed as the original nails could be pushed into their holes.

2 The mirror was cleaned (see page 42) and non-drip candles were placed in the holders. The eyelet was screwed into the last gilded ball and threaded through the chain, which was hung from the eagle's beak. Research told us that this tradition was an allusion to the cannon balls fired from battleships of the period or, more prosaically, a way of keeping flies away from both the glass and gilding.

Patination

See page 107, incorporating dust and dirt reserved after cleaning. This process was left until last to make it easier to blend the new gilding successfully with the old.

THREE - PIECE
DESK SUITE

This 1870s Louis Philippe piece, consisting of a walnut-veneered writing table, pigeon-hole shelves and wall-mounted cabinet, was found looking very sorry for itself on the pavement of a Paris flea-market. Judging by the water stains and peeling veneer, it had been left out in the rain. One section of veneer was missing, the joints were adrift, and a back leg curved awkwardly inwards. Sadly, the old, slightly rippled glass on one of the cabinet doors was broken and, experience told us, might be hard to replace: flat new glass on an old piece can look ill-matched and characterless. More off-putting were signs of woodworm on the table – when sharply tapped, a small cloud of dust was emitted, indicating that worms were perhaps still active. We were swayed, however, by the modest, antique charm of the piece, its multi-purpose possibilities and, due to its forlorn state, the rock-bottom price. Not to mention the hugely satisfying prospect of polishing the walnut to a glorious sheen!

JOB LIST

Treat woodworm / clean and strip / consolidate joints and back leg / repair and replace veneer / replace broken glass / French polish

MATERIALS

Treating the woodworm ▶ 500ml proprietary insecticide
Cleaning ▶ approx. 500ml white spirit
Stripping ▶ 1 litre solvent-based paint stripper / 2tbsp white spirit
Consolidating the joints ▶ 100ml hot pearl glue (see page 45)
Repairing and replacing veneer ▶ 0.8mm matching walnut veneer (see page 16) / 50ml hot pearl glue
Replacing the glass ▶ 250g glaziers' putty (see page 41, Glass) / 1 sheet old glass / 12mm panel pins
French polishing (see page 94) ▶ 200ml 'pure' polish / 200ml '50/50' polish / 2tsp linseed oil / 100ml methylated spirits / 100ml colourless beeswax

EQUIPMENT

Plastic sheeting / newspaper / industrial gloves / goggles / mask / camera cleaner / 15mm household paint brush / 4 syringes with needles (see page 29) / medium wirewool (grade 0) / 25mm household paint brush / blunted paint knife / coarse wirewool (grade 2) / lint-free cotton rags / rubber hammer / household sponge / hairdryer / bowl and saucepan for warming glue / small glue brush / webbing clamps / sash clamps / wood offcuts / G-clamps / large cotton cloth / electric iron / veneer hammer / greaseproof paper / 2 flat boards / weights / screwdriver / card to 'file' screws / sheet / old paring chisel / mallet / locking tape measure / steel rule / cardboard for template / craft knife / pin hammer / putty knife / 180-grade sandpaper / 2 rubbers and storage jars (see pages 95 and 96) / 180-grade silicone-carbide paper / superfine wirewool (grade 0000)

THREE - PIECE DESK SUITE

METHOD

Treating the woodworm

ALWAYS WEAR GLOVES, GOGGLES AND MASK WHEN USING INSECTICIDE. See page 36. The piece was to be restored in an unfurnished apartment with wooden parquet floors so additional measures were needed. We covered the floors with plastic sheeting and newspaper, and, once the initial treatment was complete, we turned the table upside down on the work bench, inserted syringes into each upturned leg and left them until all the liquid had been absorbed (2 weeks). The saturated table was then left to dry (1 week).

Cleaning

All surfaces were cleaned with white spirit, using medium wirewool to remove the ingrained dirt (see page 38).

Stripping

The finish proved too badly stained to retain so the piece was stripped and then neutralized with white spirit (see page 39).

Consolidating the joints

The glue holding the table section had deteriorated due to humidity and was now past reconstitution. As a result the back legs and cross rails needed total regluing. In addition, for a quick sale, plaster-based filler had been jammed into cracks between mortise and tenon joints to give an illusion of stability. Both glue and filler had to be removed before consolidation could begin.

1 The piece was carefully dismantled, using a rubber hammer to prise it gently apart (see page 43).

2 The surfaces that were to be re-glued were cleaned, using hot water, the household sponge and (occasionally) the blunted paint knife, dried with rags, and left for 1 hour.

3 All the joints were re-glued (see page 46), re-assembled, secured with webbing, sash, and G-clamps (see page 47), and left to dry (12 hours).

Although the curved back leg was now marginally straighter, we could not counteract the warping (common in walnut furniture) without cutting the leg into sections, doweling it and re-gluing. In furniture restoration the question must sometimes be asked: does the piece merit the spending of a considerable amount of work and time? In this case the desk was now stable, its modest appearance enhanced by re-veneering, and the weight of the bookcase would be evenly distributed. A certain quaint disparity was acceptable.

Repairing and replacing veneer

1 For repairing the peeling veneer on the table top, see pages 93 and 89 (Removing and Reusing Old Veneer and Hammer Veneering). Since the surface had originally been prepared with jack and toothing planes, there was no need to use either again. The top was left to dry (12 hours).

2 The veneer missing on the side of the cabinet revealed the poplar frame beneath. The new piece of walnut veneer was also applied using the hammer technique (see page 89) – again there was no need to plane. It too was left to dry for 12 hours.

Replacing the glass

We were delighted to find some old glass of a suitable size in a salvage yard. This proved a much more convincing match for the remaining original panel than any modern replacement.

1 The door was unscrewed from the cabinet and placed on the work bench, which had been covered with newspaper and an old sheet, folded to form a pad. The screws were pushed through card and labelled for reuse once the glass had been replaced.

2 The old putty and remaining glass were gently removed, using the chisel and the mallet.

3 The aperture was measured and a cardboard template made for the replacement glass, allowing a 3mm gap all round for the new putty, which had been chosen to match as closely as possible the surrounding wood.

4 Once the putty had been softened by rolling it between the hands, it was formed into strips, ready for use.

5 Cut to measure by a professional, the glass was carefully secured inside the frame, using eight panel pins.

6 Strips of putty were firmly pressed inside the frame by hand, and the putty knife was then used to neaten and bevel them. Although the putty took a month to dry completely, the door was re-screwed onto the cabinet after a week.

French polishing

1 The piece was lightly sanded, using 180-grade sandpaper, and dusted thoroughly with dampened rags.

2 See page 94 for French polishing: the whole process took 4 days, and the piece was left to dry (1 week).

3 A final protective coat of colourless beeswax was applied with superfine wirewool (see page 97, Cutting the Shine).

DRESSING TABLE

Charming little dressing tables are not much in vogue these days, but this one found a perfect home in a country house we were furnishing for clients. A 19th-century copy of an 18th-century piece, its structure was sound despite a fragile appearance. However, previous owners had covered it with inappropriate white eggshell paint and the flip-top mirror (thankfully, the glass was mercury-backed for that 'period' feel) opened to reveal a strident blue interior. We decided to repaint and distress it, adapting traditional methods for the oil-based surfaces and creating a desirable 'antique' look.

JOB LIST

Test strip / clean / sand / repaint and distress ready-painted exterior / drag blue interior

MATERIALS

Test strip ▸ 1tsp white spirit / 1tsp methylated spirits
Cleaning ▸ 250ml white spirit
Painting the exterior ▸ 1 litre white eggshell paint / artists' oil colours: 2 dashes raw umber, 2 dashes yellow ochre, 2 dashes lamp black, 2 dashes raw sienna / 4tbsp white spirit (4 coats)
Dragging the interior ▸ 250ml light blue eggshell paint / 1 dash lamp black artists' oil colour / 1tbsp white spirit

EQUIPMENT

Cotton buds / spirit-resistant vinyl gloves / lint-free cotton rags / medium wirewool (grade 0) / 150-grade sandpaper / 5 jam jars / clean 40mm varnish brush / 220-grade wet-and-dry sandpaper / masking tape / scissors

DRESSING TABLE

METHOD

Test strip
See page 38. A strip test with white spirit revealed no change, just discoloration from old wax deposits. We then tried methylated spirts to see if the paint was acrylic based. Again there was no change so we deduced that both paints were oil based. Slight surface undulations corresponding to the position of an edge-banding indicated that the surface had originally been inlaid veneer, but the client's requirements and a disinclination to confront the rigours of stripping this delicate piece were two reasons not to restore the original surface.

Cleaning

The whole table was wiped down, using rags and white spirit, to remove the old wax. Wirewool lifted the more deeply ingrained deposits.

Sanding

The little table had an uneven, rippled surface which, we felt, contributed to its 'country' appeal. The very light sanding we gave it, using 150-grade paper in a circular motion, was not, therefore, an attempt to smooth the surface but to increase the adhesion of the new paint. The piece was then dusted with damp lint-free rags.

Painting the exterior

See page 110 (Adapting for Oil-Based Painted Surfaces), for the painting and distressing techniques. Unusually, the paint was applied using a clean varnish brush for a fine finish.

1 For the first coat, 250ml eggshell paint was poured into a jam jar and, stirring well, tinted with raw umber, yellow ochre, lamp black and raw sienna for a light mouse colour, then thinned to double-cream consistency with white spirit.

2 The remaining three coats were each mixed separately and progressively lighter than the one before.

Dragging the interior

1 The bright blue eggshell interior was rubbed down, using wet-and-dry sandpaper in a circular motion, and then dusted with damp rags. The mirror was masked to protect from paint splashes – it was removed before drying began.

2 In the fifth jam jar the lamp black oil colour was stirred into the light blue eggshell, diluted with white spirit and mixed.

3 All surfaces were dragged with the varnish brush – drawn from side to side in continous strokes – to achieve an attractively uneven, striped effect and left to dry (24 hours).

ARTS AND CRAFTS
CHAIR

This simple, well-made chair, typical of the designs manufactured from the 1900s by progressive, Arts and Crafts inspired companies such as the London-based Heal and Son, was found on a skip. It had lost its drop-in seat: doubtless the former owner, underestimating the chair's unassuming lines and homely oak frame, had calculated that getting a replacement seat made would cost more than the chair was worth. We knew from research – helped by the still intact manufacturer's label visible on the back rail – that this was a mass-produced design. But close inspection revealed that not only was the chair hand-carved, it was also assembled using traditional mortise and tenon joints as opposed to the dowel joints which had become commonplace in mass-production by 1900. This indicated that the chair was possibly a prototype and therefore even worthier of rescue.

The oil and wax finish customary for this style had been smothered with a thick coat of what looked like varnish, probably in the 1930s, when easy maintenance became important. This had crazed – an indication that the original surface had not been removed. Our aim was to strip the chair carefully and re-wax without losing its original aspect.

JOB LIST

Test strip / strip / re-wax / make drop-in seat frame / upholster

MATERIALS

Test strip ▶ 1tsp white spirit / 1tsp methylated spirits / 1tsp solvent-based paint stripper
Stripping ▶ 500ml solvent-based paint stripper / 3tbsp white spirit
Re-waxing ▶ 50ml bleached (white) wax
Making the seat frame ▶ 20 x 50mm planed, straight-grained beech / 2tbsp hot pearl glue (see page 45)
Upholstery ▶ 2½m x 5cm webbing / ½m x 130cm heavyweight hessian / upholsterer's nylon thread / 350g sifted coconut fibre / 350g polished black fibre / ½m x 140cm shredded cotton wadding / ½m x 140cm polyester wadding / ½m x 140cm calico / 1m x 140cm top fabric

EQUIPMENT

Cotton buds / industrial gloves / 25mm household paint brush / blunted paint knife / synthetic abrasive pad / lint-free cotton rags / 2 stiff shoe brushes / steel rule / sliding bevel / tenon saw / try square / paring chisel / jack plane / hairdryer / heatproof bowl and saucepan for warming glue / small glue brush / G-clamps / wood offcuts for clamping / hand-held staple gun / webbing stretcher / scissors / tape measure / curved upholsterer's needle / regulator

METHOD

Test strip

See page 38. Although we were 99 per cent sure that the finish was varnish, we made a test strip, using white spirit, methylated spirits and solvent stripper and were proved right.

Stripping

See page 39. Stray wirewool filaments can blacken oak so we removed the stripper with a synthetic pad (reserving the knife for corners) and neutralized the surface with white spirit.

Re-waxing

Stripping did, as expected, remove all wax but the underlying oil, part of the original finish, had sunk deep into the grain and was intact. Bleached (white) wax was applied to reinstate the appropriate look (see page 122, steps 1–3).

Making the seat frame

1 The planed beech was measured, marked and cut into four pieces to correspond to the sides of the seat rebate.

2 The try square, sliding bevel and steel rule were used to mark, in pencil, each acute-angled half joint (see page 44).

3 The sections to be removed were shaded in pencil and then cut out, using the tenon saw.

4 The frame was dry assembled and checked for fit within the chair rebate. This is an essential part of the process because old or hand-made chairs are not always symmetrical.

5 Minor adjustments were made using the paring chisel until all the angles of the frame fitted snugly into the rebate.

6 The frame was returned to the work surface and hot pearl glue (see page 46) was brushed onto both faces of each joint. The joints were then reassembled, secured with the G-clamps (see page 47) and left to dry (12 hours).

7 The frame was checked again for fit within the rebate. A gap of 1–2mm on each side was needed to allow space for our fabric to pass over the frame so this was the right stage at which to reduce the frame slightly, using a jack plane. Never reduce frames too early because dimensions are easily misjudged and a frame cut too small is difficult to enlarge.

6 Raw edges which could cut into the fabric were bevelled with the jack plane.

Upholstery

See page 72. Ideally we would have liked to recycle a textile of the period. After a fruitless search, however, we opted for one of the readily available reproductions of a William Morris fabric, in perfect harmony with the spirit of the chair.

CHARLES EAMES
LOUNGE CHAIR

The late 1940s and '50s were extraordinary years for furniture design in North America. Advances in manufacturing technology (often a by-product of wartime aircraft and naval research), the influx of gifted designers and architects from Europe (many closely linked to the German Bauhaus movement), and the unfettered and inventive use of new materials were all factors that contributed to American excellence in the design field.

The Lounge Chair, designed in 1956 by Charles Eames and manufactured by Herman Miller, epitomizes the very best of this mid-century style, comprising a quintessentially modern structure of three steamed and moulded plywood shells mounted on a swivelling, five-pronged, cast-aluminium base combined with more traditional elements, such as rosewood veneer and sumptuous down-filled leather cushions. Its stylish good looks, generous scale and supreme comfort – it comes with matching ottoman – make this a 'must-have' for any furniture buff. The curved veneer does have a tendency, however, to work loose and break off. This was the case with a chair an architect friend recently brought to us for repair – a section of veneer on the seat shell was missing. It also needed cleaning. Note that restoration of contemporary furniture often requires a different approach and working order from that used for older pieces.

JOB LIST
Dismantle / clean veneer / replace missing
veneer / seal new veneer / clean metal and
leather / re-assemble / wax

CHARLES EAMES LOUNGE CHAIR

MATERIALS

Cleaning veneer ▶ 2 tbsp white spirit
Replacing missing veneer ▶ 0.8mm straight-grain Santos rosewood
veneer / 50ml hot pearl glue (see page 45)
Sealing new veneer ▶ 50ml proprietary white shellac polish (see page 33)
Cleaning and waxing ▶ 2tbsp methylated spirits / small tin saddle soap /
100ml lanolin-rich hide food / 50ml micro-crystalline wax

EQUIPMENT

Soft brush / Philips no. 3 screwdriver / card to 'file' screws / lint-free
cotton rags / G-clamps / wood offcuts for clamping / steel rule / craft
knife / dental scraper / sheet A2 tracing paper / veneer saw / low-tack
masking tape / low-angled block plane / 2 old cotton pillowcases / ½ bucket
dry, fine sand / ½m twine / heatproof bowl and saucepan for warming
glue / small glue brush / household sponge / electric iron / veneer hammer /
wide greaseproof paper / 18mm plywood board / deep-throat G-clamp /
superfine wirewool (grade 0000) / rubber and storage jar (see pages 95
and 96 / cottonwool / soft cloth

METHOD
Dismantling

After an initial dusting, the leather cushions were unhooked
and the three curved shells and metal pedestal were
separated. Care was taken to use the right screwdriver – as
with many modern pieces the screws form an integral part of
the design and any damage would be detrimental. The
screws were mounted on cardboard awaiting re-assembly.

Cleaning veneer

The veneer was wiped down with a rag moistened with
white spirit to remove any build-up of silicone polish.

**Replacing curved
veneer**

The sharply jagged edges where the wedge-shaped piece of
missing veneer had been were typical of breaks in rosewood,
which is brittle and splinters easily. It was necessary to even
up these edges ready for the new veneer insert.

1 Using two G-clamps cushioned with wood offcuts, the
flexible steel rule was positioned around the curve to serve
as a guide when trimming the edges with the craft knife.

2 All the old glue was laboriously removed, using the dental
scaper – the inevitably roughened surface was a useful 'key'.
We decided to substitute reversible hot pearl glue because
modern adhesives had obviously proved unsatisfactory.

3 The area of the replacement piece was traced onto tracing
paper, and the new piece cut accordingly with the veneer
saw. A dry run was made for fit, using masking tape to hold
the veneer in position, and minor adjustments were carried
out with the low-angled block plane.

4 See page 92 for preparing the 'sandbag clamps' – securing
new veneer on curved surfaces requires a departure from the
usual technique.

5 Once the sandbag was ready, the groundwork was glued and the veneer laid, heated and hammered (see page 89), working with the grain.

6 The surface was wiped clean and clamped immediately (see page 92).

7 When the bag was removed, we could see that a small section of the edge had not adhered – a common problem. This was corrected by placing the medium-hot iron on the repair for a further 30 seconds to re-form the glue. That section was re-clamped, using a G-clamp, and left to dry (12 hours).

Sealing new veneer

The original veneer had probably been spray lacquered with cellulose. It was impractical to reproduce this industrial finish in the workshop on a mere insert so we opted instead for a substitute – a proprietary bleached shellac polish.

1 After cutting the surface with superfine wirewool, two thin coats of shellac polish were applied to the new veneer with the rubber, leaving 3 hours between coats (see page 98, Substitutions).

2 The insert was then cut again gently with the wirewool for a matt effect.

Cleaning, assembly and waxing

1 The aluminium pedestal was cleaned with cottonwool moistened with methylated spirits.

2 See page 41 for cleaning and feeding the leather.

3 Once the three shells and pedestal were re-assembled, all surfaces, excluding the cushions, were polished with micro-crystalline wax.

LIST OF SUPPLIERS

If you have difficulty finding any of the specialized materials and equipment, consult the list below. ✉ Indicates that a mail-order service is available. However, bear in mind that some suppliers will not dispatch toxic or inflammable materials by post. Please note: until 22 April 2000 the new area code for central and outer London, 020, must be used by all those dialling from within London.

Axminster Power Tool Centre ✉
Chard Street
Axminster
Devon EX13 5DZ
telesales 0800 371 822
fax 0345 585 290
www.axminster.co.uk
Comprehensive range of tools for the woodworker

B. & M. (Latex) Sales Ltd ✉
73 Station Road
Addlestone
Surrey KT15 2AP
01932 847793
http://www.scoot.co.uk./b&m/
Hair and fibre fillings and wool wadding

John Bell & Croyden Ltd ✉
50–4 Wigmore Street
London W1H 0AU
020 7935 5555
Syringes and needles

John Boddy's Fine Wood and Tool Store Ltd ✉
Riverside Saw Mills
Boroughbridge
N. Yorkshire Y051 9LJ
01423 322 370
e-mail: info@john-boddy-fwts.co.uk
Wood finishes (shellac, lacquer, varnish, etc.) and joinery tools

L. Cornelissen & Son Ltd ✉
105 Great Russell Street
London WC1B 3RY
020 7636 1045
Traditional paints and pigments, rabbit-skin glue and brushes. Knowledgeable and helpful staff

J. Crispin & Son ✉
92 Curtain Road
London EC2A 3AA
020 7739 4857
www.j-crispin.mcmail.com
Veneers, stringing, inlays, veneering tools and pearl glue

The Easy Chair Company ✉
30 Lyndhurst Road
Worthing
West Sussex BN11 2DF
01903 201081
e-mail: easy chair@btinternet.com
Upholstery materials and tools

Foxell & James Ltd ✉
57 Farringdon Road
London EC1M 3JB
020 7405 0152
Paints, wood finishes and restoration materials. Excellent professional advice

John Lawrence & Co. Ltd ✉
Granville Street
Dover
Kent CT16 2LF
01304 201 425
Wide range of brass fittings

Liberon Waxes Ltd ✉
Mountfield Industrial Estate
Learoyd Road
New Romney
Kent TN28 8XU
01797 367 5555
Comprehensive range of wood finishing and restoration materials, particularly waxes

John Myland Ltd ✉
80 Norwood High Street
West Norwood
London SE27 9NW
020 8670 9161
www.mylands.co.uk
Pigments, glues, wood finishes and rottenstone

Picreator Enterprises Ltd ✉
44 Park View Gardens
Hendon NW4 2PN
020 8202 8972
Concentrated technical soap, micro-crystalline wax and a wide range of conservation materials. First-class professional advice

H.E. Savill ✉
9-12 St Martin's Place
Scarborough
N. Yorkshire YO11 2QH
01723 373 032
Wide range of accurate reproduction metal fittings. Extremely useful catalogue

Stuart R. Stevenson ✉
68 Clerkenwell Road
London EC1M 5QA
020 7253 1693
Gilding, fine-art and conservation products, including concentrated technical soap and rabbit-skin glue. Stuart Stevenson is a leading authority on gilding.

Thanet Tool Supplies ✉
New Ashford Market
Monument Way
Sevinton
Ashford TN24 0HB
01233 501 010
www.thanettools.com
Power and specialist woodworking tools. Friendly, helpful advice.

Alec Tiranti Ltd ✉
27 Warren Street
London W1P 5DG
020 7636 8565
mail order: 0118 930 2775
www.tiranti.co.uk
Sculpturing supplies, including moulding, casting and wood-carving materials

Wemyss-Houlès
40 Newman Street
London WIP 3PA
020 7255 3305
Furnishing braids, including a wide range of gimping

BIBLIOGRAPHY

Beard, Geoffrey. *The National Trust Book of English Furniture*, Penguin Books, Harmondsworth, 1986.

Bonham/MacDonald/Porter. *Victorian Interior Design*, Crescent Books, New York, 1991.

Chippendale, Thomas. *The Gentleman and Cabinet-maker's Director*, Dover, New York, 1966.

Jackson, Albert, & Day, David. *Collin's Complete Woodworker's Manual*, Collins, London, 1989.

James, David. *Upholstery Restoration*, Guild of Master Craftsman Publications, Lewes, 1997.

Lincoln, William Alexander. *The Complete Manual of Wood Veneering*, Stobart Davies, Hertford, 1984.

Mayer, Ralph. *The Artist's Handbook of Materials and Techniques*, Faber & Faber, London, 5th edition, 1991.

Metropolitan Museum of Art. *Period Rooms in the Metropolitan Museum of Art*, Harry N. Abrams Inc., New York, 1996.

Pradère, Alexandre. *French Furniture Makers*, Sotheby's Publications, London, 1989.

Praz, Mario. *Illustrated History of Interior Decoration*, Thames and Hudson, London, 1982.

SHORT COURSES FOR AMATEUR RESTORERS

Castle Workshops
Château de Lucens
Lucens 1522
Switzerland
tel/fax 0041 21 906 8033

West Dean College
West Dean, Chichester
West Sussex PO18 0QZ
01243 811 301

INDEX

A

abrasives, 31, 32, 40
African mahogany,
    18–19, 135, 146
aged paint finish:
    glue tempera paint,
        108–11
    on oil-based paint, 110
American mahogany, *see*
    cherry
American walnut, 20–1
antiques:
    buying, 8, 138
    dating, 10–11, 78
    definition of, 9
    recognizing, 10
antiquing:
    gilding 107
    paint, 110
    see also patinating
Armenian bole, *see* bole
Arts and Crafts chair,
    restoring, 165–7
ash, 18–19
auctions:
    catalogues, 8
    ceiling price, 8

B

back plate, moulding,
    67–9
beech, 18–19, 36, 37,
    53, 112, 129
beeswax, 33
    sticks, 33, 87
    using, 122–3
bichromate of potash,
    using, 113–14
birch, 18–19
black water marks, 83
blooming, 83
bole, 103–4, 105, 107
bracket foot, replacing,
    62–3
brass:
    cleaning, 42
    drawer handles, 67
burl walnut, 20–1
burns, patching, 83, 87
burr walnut, veneering
    with, 88
butterfly keys, 55

C

cane:
    cleaning and stripping,
        41
    mending, 53
carnauba wax, 33, 122
Carrara marble, cream,
    120

case furniture, 62
castors, 67
cedar, 20–1,115
cellulose lacquer,
    repairing, 98
Cennini, Cennino, 100
chairs, 37, 48
    Arts and Crafts,
        restoring, 165–7
    broken end of leg,
        gluing, 50
    broken end of leg,
        replacing, 50–1
    broken mortise joint,
        mending, 51–2
    broken stretcher,
        replacing, 48
    Charles Eames,
        restoring, 168–71
    dining, restoring, 126–9
    feet, buttons on, 49
    joining broken leg, 52–3
    leather, restoring, 78–9
    legs, evening up, 49
    neoclassical repro,
        restoring, 54
    replacing under-seat
        blocks, 52
    sabre-leg, restoring,
        138–41
    seat frame, replacing,
        167
    see also tables, tripod,
        carving new leg for;
        upholstery
Charles Eames Lounge
    Chair, restoring, 168–71
cherry, 18–19, 112
chests of drawers:
    bracket foot, replacing,
        62–3
    drawer base, repairing,
        64
    evolution of, 62
    foot, regluing, 152–3
    late 18th c., restoring,
        150–3
    stringing, replacing,
        153
    support blocks, adding
        to base, 62
    worn drawer sides,
        repairing, 66
    worn runners on
        drawers, replacing, 65
    see also tables,
        buttterfly keys, joining
Chippendale, Thomas, 19
chisels and gouges, 25
cigarette burns, 83
clamping, 23, 28, 47
    alternatives to, 47, 91,
        92

curved veneer, of, 92
    improvised, 28, 52
    inside the carcase, 65
clay bole, *see* bole
cleaning, 23
    brass, of, 42
    cane, of, 41
    faux bois on, 18th c.
        chest of drawers, 152
    gilded wood, of, 41
    glass, of, 41
    leather, of, 41
    marble, of, 42
    mirrors, of, 42
    ormolu, of, 42
    over-zealous, 38
    wood finishes, of, 38–9
coach-lining, 141
concentrated technical
    soap, 38, 41, 42
consolidation, 23
    clamps, using, 47
    dismantling furniture,
        43–5
    gluing, 45–7
    structural repair, extent
        of, 43
    see also chairs; tables;
        chests of drawers
copies, spotting, 10–11
Country style, 8
cracks:
    major, joining, 55
    minor, filling, 86–7
craft knife, 24, 25, 27
crazing, 83
Cuban mahogany, 16,
    18–19

D

death watch beetle,
    treating, 36
dents, repairing, 85
desks:
    leather-topped, restoring,
        125, 134–7
    three-piece, restoring,
        158–61
dining chair, restoring,
    126–9
dismantling furniture, 10,
    23, 43–5
    Charles Eames chair, 170
    restored, 44–5
    tambour door, jammed,
        148
    unrestored, 43–4
dovetail joints:
    cutting, 59
    dismantling, 44
dowel joints:
    cutting, 60

dismantling, 44, 48,
    gluing, 54
dragging, 164
drawers:
    base, repairing, 64
    brass handles, 67
    development of, 64, 65
    worn runners, replacing,
        65
    worn sides, repairing, 66
    see also metal fittings
dressing table, restoring,
    162–4
drop-in seat:
    replacing seat frame, 167
    replacing upholstery, 77–8

E

18th c. chest of drawers,
    restoring, 150–3
electric drill, 24
Empire-style furniture, 17
Empire-style night table,
    restoring, 146–9
European walnut, 20–1

F

fakes, recognizing, 10
faux bois see graining
finishing, 32–3
    aged paint, 108–11
    French polishing, 94–9
    gilding, 103–9
    graining, 116–18
    marbling, 119 –21
    oil and wax, 165, 167
    staining, 112–15
    wax on wood, 122–3
French polishing, 88, 94
    bodying up, 96–7
    butts and burls, 99
    charging rubber, 95
    denibbing, 96
    fadding, 96
    materials and
        equipment, 94
    protecting, 97
    repairing, 82, 83, 85, 98
    rubber, making, 95
    shellac polish as
        varnish, 98
    shine, cutting, 97
    spiriting off, 96
    substituting, 98
    see also shellac

G

gate-leg table,
    replacing chassis on,
        56–7

INDEX

gesso, 40–1, 100, 108
  applying, 102, 132, 141, 157
  discoloured, 100
  mixing, 101
  patching with, 102
  removing, 132
  under oil-based paint, 41
  wet polishing, 102
  see also rabbit-skin glue size
gilded mirror, restoring, 154–7
gilded wood, cleaning, 41
gilding, 103
  antiquing, 107
  applying, 157
  bole, 107
  burnishing, 105
  faulting, 104
  leaf, applying, 104
  leaf, handling, 35
  materials, 35
  oil gilding, 105, 106–7
  patinating, 107
  surface, priming, 103
  tools, 34–5
  water gilding, 103–5, 107
  water marks, avoiding, 104
glass:
  cleaning and repairs, 41
  replacement, 161
glue:
  hot pearl glue, 45
  modern glues, 44, 45
  pots for heating, 46
  rabbit-skin glue, 35, 101–1
  traditional, removing, 38–9
  see also glue tempera paint; size
gluing, 23, 43
  hot pearl glue, making and using, 46–7
  joints, strengthening, 47
  PVA, on leather, 79
  rubbing in, 62
  'starved' joints, 47
  using clamps, 46, 47
  veneer, 47, 89
  wood to metal, 157
  see also clamping
gold leaf:
  loose leaf, 35, 104–5
  transfer leaf, 35, 105, 106
Gothic Revival, 8
gouache, 30, 145

gouges, 25
graining, 87, 116
  mahogany, 118
  oak, 118
  protecting, 118
  walnut, 116–18

H
half joints, dismantling, 44
hammers, 25, 43, 44
  see also tools, veneering, for; tools, upholstery, for
hammer veneering 89–90
handles, 67
hardwood, 14, 18–21, 94
hazardous materials, handling, 29
heat gun, 43, 45, 46
Hepplewhite, George, 21
hinges, 67
  pivot, replacing, 70
'Historismus' style, 78
Honduras mahogany, 18–19
hot pearl glue, see glue; gluing

I
infestation, 36
  damaged furniture, repairing, 37
  woodworm, testing, 23, 36
  woodworm, treating, 36, 160
ink stains, 83

J
jigsaw, 24, 59
joints:
  cutting, 24, 25, 50–2, 56–7, 59, 60
  dismantling, 43–4, 45
  strengthening with glue, 47
jubilee clip, 28, 52–3

K
key:
  handle, replacing, 71
  ward lock, for, replacing, 70–1
knobs, replacing, 23
knuckle joints:
  cutting, 56–7
  dismantling, 44

L
laburnum, 16
leather:
  chair, mending, 78–9
  cleaning and repair, 41–2
  top, replacing, 41–2
leather-topped desk, restoring, 125, 134–7
locks, 67
  escutcheon, moulding, see back plate
loose joints:
  cause of, 37, 39, 47
  treating, 37, 43, 47

M
macassar, 20–1
mahogany, 43, 55, 66, 94
  African, 18–19, 125, 134–7
  Cuban, 18–19
  Honduras, 18–19
  staining, 112, 114
marble, cleaning and repairs, 42
marbled top table, restoring, 130–3
marbling, 7, 119
  cream Carrara, 120
  rosso di Verona, 121
  verde–nero, 119–20
measuring and marking, 24
metal fittings:
  antiquing, 69
  back plate, moulding, 67–9
  brass handles, 67
  key for ward lock, making, 70–1
  pivot hinge, replacing, 70
  purpose of, 67
Metropolitan Museum, New York, 8
micro-crystalline wax, 41, 69
mildew on wood, see mould
mirrors:
  cleaning and repairs, 42
  gilded, restoring, 154–7
missing inlay, replacing, 92
mortise and tenon joints, 43–4, 48
  repairing mortise, 51–2, 52–3
moulding, replacing, 136, 145
mould on wood, 37

N
nails, removing 25, 44–5
neoclassical chair, repairing, 54
nitro stains, using, 114–15, 137

O
oak, 15, 18–19, 66
  abrasives on, 31
  maturity, 14
  'scorch' marks, curing, 83
  staining, 112–13
olive, 16
orange-peel effect, 85
ormolu, cleaning, 42

P
paint, 30
  aged, 108–11, 133
  French cream, 109
  gouache, 30
  oil, 30
  powder pigment, 30
  preparing for, 40
  Swedish blue, 108-11
paint brushes, 30–1
painted washstand, restoring, 142–5
painting techniques:
  coach-lining, 141
  dragging, 164
  graining, 116–18
  marbling, 119–21
  preparing for, 40–1
  see also aged paint
paintwork, restoring, 141, 143
patina:
  importance of, 38, 82
  protection of, 136
patinating, 107
period furniture, assessing, 10–11
Phyfe, Duncan, 21
pine, 20, 36, 66, 115, 116
  dents in, repairing, 85
  stained, French polishing of, 94
pinned tenon joints, dismantling, 43–4
pivot hinge, replacing, 70
planes, 26
  see also tools, veneering
powder pigment, 30
powder-post beetle, treating, 36
projects:
  Arts and Crafts chair, 165–7

Charles Eames Lounge
Chair, 168–71
chest of drawers,
150–3
dining chair, 126–9
dressing table, 162–4
Empire-style night table,
146–9
gilded mirror, 154–7
leather chair, 78–9
leather-topped
mahogany desk, 125,
134–7
neoclassical chair, 54
painted washstand,
142–5
regency sabre-leg chair,
138–41
regency table, 60
'Swedish' stool, 110–11
table with marbled top,
130–3
three-piece desk suite,
158–61
tripod table, 84–5
walnut table, 99
protective clothing, 29
Provincial style, 8
pseudo mahogany, see
African mahogany

R

rabbit-skin glue size,
100–1
red rot, see leather,
cleaning and repairs
Regency sabre-leg chair,
restoring, 138–41
Regency table, restoring
60
reproduction furniture,
recognizing, 10
restoration:
change in concept of,
6–7
furniture in need of,
buying, 8
irreversible, 39
organizing project, 23
reversibility, 22, 37, 40,
45, 105, 141
structural repairs, extent
of, 43, 82, 143, 156,
160
wood for, buying,
14–16
work space, 24, 29
Revival style, 8, 78
reviver, making and
applying, 82
rosewood, 20–1, 43, 60,
115, 116, 168

rosso di Verona marble,
121
rot, see wood rot

S

safety precautions, 25,
29, 39
sanding, 32
satinwood, 20–1, 60
saws, 25
see also tools, veneering
'scorch' marks on oak, 83
scratches, filling, 86–7
screwdrivers, 26
screws, removing, 25, 26,
44–5
seat frame, replacing, 167
second-hand furniture,
buying, 8
Shaker furniture, 6
shellac, 33
proprietary polishes, 33,
94
sticks, 32, 33, 87
substituting for modern
finishes, 98
varnish, polish as, 98,
141
see also French polishing
size, see rabbit-skin glue
size
softwood, 14, 20–1
dents in, 85
soldering iron, 87
spirit stains, 83
splice joint, 50–1
spokeshaves, 26
staining, 39, 112
bichromate of potash,
using, 113–14
matching, 112
nitro stains, using,
114–15
ready-made stains, 112
vandyke brown crystals,
using, 112–13
stains, spirit and ink, 83
see also water marks,
white
staple gun, 34, 72
stool, 'Swedish',
restoring, 110–11
stringing, replacing, 92,
153
stripping, 23
cane, 41
caustic dipping, 39
concealing 'patchwork'
effect of, 39
dry stripping, 39
French polish, partial, 98
over water gilding, 156

safety precautions, 39
using solvent-based
paint stripper, 40, 132
test, 38, 140, 156, 164,
167
wood finishes, of, 39–40
stuff-over seat, replacing,
72–6
surface repairs, 82
black water marks, 83
blooming, 83
burns, patching, 87
cigarette burns, 83
cracks and scratches,
minor, 55, 86–7
crazing, 83
dents, 85
dull finish, 83
ink stains, 83
orange-peel effect, 85
reviver, making and
applying, 82
scorch marks, 83
spirit stains, 83
stains, bleaching, 86
sun bleached, 85
white water marks, 83
worn edges, 85
Swedish stool, 110–11
sycamore, 94
synthetic lacquer,
repairing, 98
syringes and needles, 29,
36, 37, 43, 44, 47

T

tables:
butterfly keys, joining
cracks with, 55
corner moulding,
replacing, 136
Empire-style night table,
restoring, 146–9
gate-leg, replacing
chassis on, 37, 56–7
leg, extending, 60
marbled top, with,
restoring, 130–3
Regency, restoring, 60
styles, evolving, 55
top, replacing, 133
tripod, carving new leg
for, 58–9
tripod, restoring, 85
walnut, French
polishing, 99
see also chairs, replacing
broken end of leg
tack holes, filling, 87
tack lifter, 34, 128
tambour door, repairing,
146, 148

test strip, see stripping
termites, treating, 36
Thonet, Michael, 19
three-piece desk suite,
restoring, 158–61
tools:
antiques, 13
buying, 24
camera cleaner, 36
chisels and gouges, 25,
45
clamps, 28
craft knife, 24, 27
electric drill, 24
gilding, for, 34–5
hand tools, 24
heat gun, 43, 45, 46
jigsaw, 24
measuring, 24
oilstone, 25, 27
planes, 26
power tools, 24
saws, 25
screwdrivers, 26, 44
soldering iron, 45, 87
spokeshaves, 26
staple gun, 34, 72
syringe, 29, 36, 37, 43,
44, 47
tack lifter, 34, 45
upholstery, for, 34–5,
72
veneering, for, 27
tripod table see table
turner, wood, 16, 48, 60

U

upholstery, 23, 34, 72
Arts and Crafts chair,
167
dating, 126
drop-in seat, replacing,
77–8
matching colour, 129
materials, 72, 77
19th c. dining chair,
128–9
removal of, 72, 128
stuff-over seat,
replacing, 72–6
tools, 34–5, 72

V

vandyke brown crystals,
using, 112–13, 114
varnish, removing, 140
varnishing, 120
marbled table top, 133
shellac, with, 98, 140
veneer:
antique, hand-sawn, 16

INDEX / ACKNOWLEDGMENTS

blisters, repairing, 91
burl cut, 17
burr cut, 17
butt cut, 17
buying, 1617
crotch cut, 17
curved, clamping, 92
curved, replacing, 170
flame cut, 17
mail-order, buying through, 16
missing inlay, replacing, 92
old, removing and reusing, 93
oyster, 16
patching, 91
replacing, 92, 153
stringing, substitute, 16
thickness, 16, 148
veneer tape, 16, 27
veneering:
burr and butt walnut, with, 88
development of, 88
drawbacks of, 88
equipment for, 27

gluing, 47
hammer, 89–90
verde-nero marble, 119–20

W

walnut, 94, 99
American, 20–1
burl, 20–1
European, 20–1
graining, 116–18
staining, 122
veneers, 88
ward lock, key for, making, 70–1
washstand, painted, restoring, 142–5
water marks:
black, 83
white, 83
wax, 88
antiquing, 108, 110
beeswax, 33
carnauba wax, 33, 122
coloured, 122–3
oil and, 165, 167
sticks, 32, 33
wood, on, 122–3

white ants, treating, 36
white water marks, 83
whiting, 30, 35, 100
Windsor chairs, 19
wirewool, 32, 38
wood finishes:
aged paint, 108–10
cleaning, 38
French polishing, 94–8
graining, 116–18
marbling, 119–21
oil gilding, 106–7
staining, 112–15
stripping, 39–40
water gilding, 103–5
waxing, 122–3
wood:
central heating, effect of, 17, 55
damp, effect of, 37
'exotic', 14, 20–1
faux bois, see graining
graining, 116–18
hardwood, 14, 18–21
identifying, 14
laying down, 16
lightening, 86
living qualities of, 17
new, buying, 14

plain sawing, 15
quarter sawn and squared, 15
recycled, 15
restoration, buying for, 14–16
reviving finishes, 82, 83
rift sawing, 15
seasoning, 14–15, 55
softwood, 14, 20–1
stains, bleaching, 86
tangential sawing, 15
turning, 16, 48, 60
unobtainable, 115
veneers, buying, 16-17
warping, 15, 17, 19, 21, 55, 144, 160
water on, effect of, 39
wax on, 122–3
wood rot:
furniture damaged by, 37
treating, 37
woodworm:
spotting, 36, 110
treating, 36, 160
workbench, 24
work space, 24, 29
worn edges, 85

AUTHORS' ACKNOWLEDGMENTS

Our sincere thanks to the many people involved in making this book: the admirable publishing team at Quadrille, in particular Mary Evans and Jane O'Shea; Mary Davies, our indefatigable editor; designer Sue Storey and photographer Patrick McLeavey, who kept their cool when we turned their studio into a workshop; Bill Batten for his wonderfully atmospheric location shots; and Louise Fontenoy in Paris, who uncomplainingly typed our copy at the strangest hours. Stuart Stevenson answered our questions well beyond the call of duty, as did Martin at Foxell & James. We are grateful to Marianne Dunn, and to Peter Gordon and Alfred for help with Upholstery. A very warm thank you to the Galerie Koller, Zurich – Pierre Koller, ever the soul of generosity; Karl Green, our favourite furniture expert, whose lectures provided the basis of 'What to look out for'; and Herr A. Ritzmann, Master Restorer. Rex Dunbar, Hugues de Melin and Yu-Chee Chong provided a great support system. Finally, special thanks to our families and to our friends at the Château de Lucens – without their help this book would not have been possible.

PICTURE ACKNOWLEDGMENTS

The publishers wish to thank the following photographers and organizations for their kind permission to reproduce photographs in this book: 6 Ljad Creyghton / Camera Press; 8 Fritz von Schulenberg / Interior Archive; 9 Jean-Paul Bonhommet / Elizabeth Whiting & Associates; and 88 Peter Woloszynski / Elizabeth Whiting & Associates.

James Bain Smith took the 'before' photographs on pages 60, 99 top, 110, 126, 130, 135, 138, 143, 155, 158, 162 and 168.

Bill Batten took the location photographs on pages 1, 2, 4, 5, 7, 10, 11, 12, 42, 54, 61, 74, 78 bottom, 79, 80, 84, 85, 99 bottom, 100, 106, 111, 123, 124, 127, 128, 131, 133, 134, 137, 139, 140, 142, 145, 146, 147, 149, 150, 153, 154, 156, 157, 159, 161, 163, 164, 166, 167, 169 and 171.

All the studio photography was by Patrick McLeavey. He also took the 'before' photographs on pages 22, 151 and 165.

The line drawings on pages 44, 71, 75 and 96 are by James Bain Smith.